Oscar Peterson

OSCAR PETERSON

Richard Palmer

Selected discography
by Richard Palmer

Spellmount
TUNBRIDGE WELLS

Hippocrene Books
NEW YORK

First published in the UK in 1984 by
SPELLMOUNT LTD
12 Dene Way, Speldhurst,
Tunbridge Wells, Kent TN3 0NX
ISBN 0 946771 45 6 (UK)

© Spellmount Ltd, 1984

Palmer, Richard
    Oscar Peterson. – (Jazz Masters)
    1. Peterson, Oscar 2. Jazz musicians – United States – Biography
    I.Title   II. Series
    785. 42'092'4 ML 419.P/

First published in the USA by
HIPPOCRENE BOOKS INC.
171 Madison Avenue,
New York, NY 10016

ISBN 0 87052 011 3 (USA)

Series editor : John Latimer Smith
Cover design : Peter Theodosiou

Printed & bound in Great Britain
by Anchor / Brendon Ltd, Tiptree, Essex

Contents

PART ONE: THE MAN   9

PART TWO: THE CAREER   15

   One: *Beginnings*   15

   Two: *Hello Herbie: The Guitar Trios, 1952–58*   21

   Three: *Drums In My Ears: 1958–71*   27

   Four: *Solo And Pablo: The Compleat Pianist*   43

   Five: *Just You, Just Me: Peterson as Accompanist*   52

   Six: *Hymn To Freedom: A Note on Peterson The Composer*   58

PART THREE: THE MUSICAL ACHIEVEMENT   65

   One: *Peterson and Tatum*   66

   Two: *The Peterson Style*   73

NOTES   76

DISCOGRAPHY   79

To Steve Voce

Abbreviations

Throughout my text I have drawn extensively on two BBC programme transcripts of interviews with Oscar Peterson. Designated references appear as explained below.

PC   'Oscar Peterson: The Compleat Pianist'. An illustrated conversation conducted by Peter Clayton and broadcast on BBC Radio 3 on 12 April, 1974.*

AP   'Oscar Peterson In Conversation With André Previn'. An illustrated musical reminiscence broadcast on *Omnibus*, BBC-TV, 11/12/74 and 14/9/75

*I would like to thank Peter Clayton, Derek Drescher, Gary Russell and, especially, Peggy Cummings, for their help in providing me with this transcript.

PART ONE: THE MAN

The requirements for glamour in jazz too often include eccentricity, limited technical scope (supposedly compensated by 'soul'), a personal background of social problems, and a tendency to show up for the Wednesday matinee at midnight on Thursday. By these standards Oscar Peterson was a cinch to be voted Least Likely to Succeed. [1]

Leonard Feather

Jazz musicians are a heterogeneous lot. They come in all shapes and sizes, from every social and economic background, from every continent and racial group. Many have died young, or been physically disadvantaged; others have had iron constitutions and enjoyed remarkable longevity. Some have been illiterate; others highly educated. Some major jazz musicians could not read music; and yet there are others who hold doctorates and other higher degrees in composition and musicology. It is therefore unwise to suggest that any particular jazz musician is 'unusual'.

Yet there are several good reasons for applying the word to Oscar Peterson. For a start, he is one of a very select group of important jazz artists who have come from Canada. Secondly, he has had a career of unbroken success: he has never known neglect either from promoters or record companies, and he has never had to worry where the next job was coming from. Thirdly, he is far more widely known than most jazz musicians. Throughout his career, he has appealed to an audience outside the specialist jazz one, and in the last decade he has also become a well-known television personality. And fourthly, he has had a notably *un*sensational private life. In an art form that can sometimes seem over-populated by figures racked by the world's indifference or their own inability to cope, Oscar Peterson stands out as the epitome of unhistrionic professionalism and salubrious maturity. Since the jazz world has always shown a tendency to lionise its victims in a seedily Romantic fashion, he is also a living provocation to those who prefer their heroes to be tragically flawed. For thirty-five years he has unfussily 'taken care of business': he has few characteristics likely to endear him to theorists who delight in the drama, scandal and fragility commonly associated with 'the artistic life'.

A minor consequence of this is that any attempt to write a critical biography (even one of this length) of a man who is 'as normal as heterosexuality, as gentlemanly as David Niven'[2] runs into a certain difficulty unusual in jazz criticism. It is as yet impossible to write about the work of, for example, Bud Powell, Charlie Parker, or Charles Mingus – unquestionably three of the most important figures in modern* jazz – *without* paying close attention to their lives. We will have to wait for at least fifty years before the music can stand free of the dramatic and often appalling circumstances that attended its making. At present, men like Powell, Parker and Mingus – and even figures like Ellington and Coltrane – are so surrounded by the mythology that their lives created, that a pure critical assessment of their work is not possible for even the most skilful biographers.

In Peterson's case, however, it is already possible to discuss his work in a properly detached way, even though he is, happily, very much alive and profusely active as a player. That is why I offer only this brief first chapter on Peterson the man: the rest of the book is devoted to an account of his career and his recorded oeuvre, which is massive. Furthermore, it should be said that Oscar, while the most friendly and approachable of men, has always kept his private life resolutely private; and I do not see it as the function of a study of this kind to pry into things that he has chosen not to make part of the public domain.

***

Oscar Emmanuel Peterson was born in Montreal, Canada, on August 15, 1925. His parents are both West Indians: his mother, a cook, came from St Kitts in the Leeward Islands, and his sailor father from the Virgin Islands. They emigrated independently to the Dominion, met and married in Montreal, and raised a family, one which turned out to be rich in musical talent. One of the daughters was to become a piano teacher: an accomplished classical pianist, she helped launch Oscar's career, and still follows it with toughly appraising love. A brother, Chuck, played the trumpet, which Oscar himself studied until an attack of tuberculosis forced him to turn to another instrument.

*The term 'modern jazz' has recently become ambiguous. Nowadays, it is often used to refer to the 'avant garde' – to Ornette Coleman and his successors. Here and throughout I use the term in its original meaning of post-1940 jazz – of the bop revolution and after.

A full account of Oscar's early development as a pianist appears in the next chapter. Here I want only to draw attention to one of the few 'unusual' facts about his life as a musician – that from his late teens he has suffered from arthritis in his hands. There is a history of the ailment in his family, and Peterson has often found it extremely painful to play. Occasionally he has had to cancel concerts because the pain is too inhibiting; but it says much for his stoicism and professional pride that he has usually fulfilled engagements even when suffering quite badly. Of course, many artists perform superbly under considerable privation; as Alistair Cooke has said, 'A professional is a man who can do his best work when he doesn't feel like it.'[3] But I have always found Peterson's almost blithe acceptance of the problem impressive: he did not even mention it in a public interview until 1975.

No account of Peterson could be complete without mentioning the vital role that Norman Granz has played in his life. It was Granz who persuaded him to come south from Canada and who then recorded him regularly; and as I shall be showing later, it was Granz's return to the recording industry in 1972 (with Pablo records) that inspired arguably the richest stage of Oscar's entire output.

Granz has over the years attracted a great deal of critical flak for the alleged excesses of his Jazz At The Philharmonic* concerts, for his liking for apparently brash, extrovert jam sessions, and for his overall 'philosophy of jazz'. I am not in agreement with these views anyway; but even his fiercest critics could not deny that Granz did a great deal for the musicians in his 'stable' – and nearly all the major musicians in jazz recorded for him at some time or another during the 19.0s. He insisted on the best treatment and the best possible money for them; he absolutely refused to play segregated audiences; and he was always sharply on the lookout for any attempt to take advantage of the players under his care. Roy Eldridge, who benefitted more than most from his patronage, once declared, 'They should make a statue to that cat, and there's no one else in the business end of this business I would say that about.'[4]

Granz has been Peterson's manager from the beginning, including all the years when he absented himself from the record business. And there

*Hereinafter referred to as JATP. 'Jazz At The Philharmonic' is taken from the venue of the first jam session concert Granz promoted, at the Los Angeles Philharmonic Auditorium on July 2, 1944.

is no doubt that his influence has been profound. Peterson's level-headedness makes it unlikely that he would have gone off the rails or failed to succeed; but Granz's careful management and imaginative use of Peterson's talent ensured that Oscar would not, in Granz's words, become 'just another saloon pianist'. Together they planned Oscar's nationwide exposure in America; and Granz soon hit on the crucial insight that Peterson would make an expert and versatile accompanist, an awareness that set up a number of marvellous sessions featuring some of the finest soloists in jazz history.

Oscar Peterson has been married three times – to Lillian, Sandy, and Charlotte. The dissolution of the first two appears to have been amicable, and Oscar is the devoted father of the six children that have come from the three marriages. In a rare comment upon his marital life he has said:

> My first marriage was simply a matter of being mismatched. I don't say that to derogate my first wife and I don't think she would take it that way. It wasn't just a question of being on the road – I was into a lot of things, a lot of projects, and she basically felt it was a little hard. And I think that at a young age it's a lot to ask of a young woman – punching maps in her face and hopping here, there and everywhere while trying to raise a family. I wouldn't do that again. . . I think I can be as difficult to live with as anyone else. Because, you know, anyone who is a performer undergoes great periods of tremendous elation and great periods of depression – they are affected, emotional. . . It really comes down to a matter of compatibility; it is a matter of whoever I'm with, understanding what I am and what I do.[5]

There is no doubt that the jazz life, with its globe-trotting, its unusual hours, and all the attendant temptations and problems, can be a very tough one, especially for a young family. Peterson has seen many of his close colleagues go under as a result – Billie Holiday, Parker, Lester Young, and the young pianist Hampton Hawes, with whom Oscar struck up an early friendship, and whom he helped in a variety of ways warmly acknowledged in Hawes autobiography. Indeed, Hawes called Peterson 'a good brother, looking after his own'.[6]

That moving tribute seems no less than Peterson deserves. He is a man whose charm and genuine friendliness amazed British television technicians, and about whom nobody in the jazz world seems to have anything but good to say. It could be argued that he has been lucky; and I know Oscar would be the first to acknowledge his good fortune in terms of health and the loving care that his family always embodied. But I would also say that his triumphant survival in a milieu littered with casualties has been *earned* – earned through intelligence, a sensible awareness of the dangers of narcotics, booze and partying that undermined so many talented contemporaries, and above all a loving devotion to the thing that made him a jazz musician in the first place – the piano.

It is this aesthetic dedication that most shines out of Peterson the man. The sheer joy and awe he has always derived from playing is his life force:

> I could never think of giving up what I'm doing. I could never, for instance, settle down and become a studio musician. That kind of job was offered to me years ago, but it doesn't represent the way I want to live. When I stop playing the way I'm playing, I'll just close the piano lid one night and stop for good.[7]

As he enters his sixtieth year, one can only hope that such a moment is still far distant, and that his boundless pleasure in creating music remains the abiding passion of his life.

PART TWO: THE CAREER

ONE
Beginnings

There's a pianist up here who's just too much. You've never heard anything like it!

Dizzy Gillespie in Montreal, 1948

Jazzmen Kenny Wheeler, Gil Evans, Maynard Ferguson, Paul Bley and Oscar Peterson seem a very disparate quintet. But they share a major characteristic: they are all Canadians.

Oscar Peterson's nationality is crucial to any assessment of his career. One reason is that his love for his homeland is an important force in his life, and was the well-spring of one of his most enduring achievements as a composer – the *Canadiana Suite*. Even more significant, perhaps, is that it explains why Oscar's formative years as a musician went unremarked, so that when he finally appeared in the United States, he burst upon the American jazz scene with the impact of a new planet.

Born and raised in Montreal, Oscar first studied trumpet, having begun his classical studies at the age of six. But some eighteen months later he contracted TB; and although he was fully cured after over a year of hospitalisation, he had to renounce any idea of playing brass or woodwind thereafter. Instead, he became the family's pianist.

The subject of Peterson's formidable technique will arise several times during this book. It is essential to understand from the outset that his exceptional facility is not a matter of some extravagant natural gift. His control over the piano, and his loving sensitivity to the instrument's grandeur, derive from dedicated work as much as inborn talent. He would practise from nine in the morning until noon; from one o'clock till six; and from seven thirty until he was 'dragged away from the keyboard so that the family could get some sleep.' Such discipline lies at the heart of Peterson's scholarly approach to his music, and it also goes a long way to explaining his achievements as an accompanist, which is a skill founded on wide-ranging musical knowledge and intelligence.

Some six years elapsed before Oscar's playing began to reflect a

15

growing interest in jazz. He has recounted to André Previn what made him move away from classical music towards being a jazz improviser:

I found that there were certain things that made me want to play them another way, which is not the way you become a good classical pianist! But, being frustrated, I'd take these classical pieces and try to move them around jazz-wise, and it didn't happen – I mean, it *can't* happen, *today*, to me or anyone. And through that I basically found out I was a player and not an interpreter. (AP)

A major fillip to his jazz studies occurred when he entered a talent contest and won the first prize of $250. He used the money to buy his own first piano.

At about this time, too, he came under the spell of the man who was to dominate his thinking and feeling about jazz, and who came to be one of his closest friends: Art Tatum. As he recalled to Previn:

My first bruising with Art Tatum came at a very tender age, in my teens. I thought I was pretty heavy at school, you know – I'd play in all the lunch hours with all the chicks round the auditorium. And my Dad was watching all this quietly, and I think he got the feeling that I was getting a little too egotistical about it; and one day he came home and said, 'Listen, there's something I want you to hear. It's a record.' And he put it on, and I'll never forget – it was Art Tatum's *Tiger Rag*. And, truthfully, I gave up the piano for two solid months; and I had crying fits at night.(AP)

The question of Peterson's musical relationship to Tatum is a large one, and I deal with it fully in Part Three. For now, it is enough to say that despite its initially discouraging effect, Tatum's impact was another major factor in weaning the young Canadian away from a possible career as a concert pianist and into the realm of jazz. His talent blossomed. He had a spell with an orchestra led by Johnny Holmes, whom Peterson credits with changing his direction and building up his technique, enabling him to evolve a distinct style. Nor was Holmes the only leader to be impressed. Oscar was not yet twenty when he received an offer from Jimmie Lunceford to join his prestigious band. He turned it down.

Why? Most young musicians would have given their eye teeth to work with Lunceford, whose reputation at this time was only marginally smaller than Ellington's or Basie's; so what made the young Peterson refuse an opportunity that must have seemed dazzling? Accounts differ. Most have argued that Peterson felt he wasn't ready yet, that he needed more time to develop a style which would have something vital and permanent to say. However, Oscar himself has said that

> I was ready to go, believe it or not, but I was still in school, and my parents were a little concerned about me. They didn't feel it was wise at that time to just burst into that environment.(PC)

I would guess that the refusal was due to a mixture of filial duty and a private suspicion that he wasn't quite mature enough musically or personally. Peterson has always been a perfectionist, his own fiercest critic and hardest task-master; and the delay in his move south (Lunceford's was not the only offer) suggests that he was determined not to go until he was certain he could cope in every way.

If America's temporary loss was Canada's gain, the word spread rapidly around the States about this youngster's talent. Coleman Hawkins heard him in 1945 and was tremendously impressed; and Leonard Feather has recalled how he failed to become the man who launched Oscar's US career. Planning a forthcoming concert, Feather got a call from and excited Dizzy Gillespie in Montreal:

> 'Leonard, there's a pianist up here who's just too much. You've never heard anything like it! We gotta put him in the concert.' I had to tell him that the budget for the concert was already excessive, and we simply couldn't afford to import an unknown.'[1]

Nine months later, Peterson *did* make his American debut. Norman Granz persuaded him to take part in a JATP concert in NYC, on September 18, 1949. He stopped the show cold in its tracks: it's worth quoting from Mike Levin's now-celebrated *Downbeat* review:

> Peterson displayed a flashing right hand, a load of bop and George Shearing-influenced ideas, as well as a good sense of harmonic development. And in addition, he scared the local modern minions by playing bop figures single-fingered in the *left* hand, which is distinctly not the common practice.[2]

There has not been a more dramatic jazz debut, unless it was Lester Young's some thirteen years previously. Curiously, however, Oscar's career did not immediately take off in the way one might anticipate after such a triumph. Undoubtedly, it *could* have done; but Peterson and

17

1 Oscar in Hans Georg Brunner-Schwer's studios (Hans Harzheim)

Granz felt it was better for him to return to Canada and take stock. In short, they *planned* his career, the kind of sober strategy that characterises many *classical* virtuosi's preparation but is very rare in the jazz world. Oscar remembers Granz putting it thus:

'Let's just cool it and see what the reaction *really* is, and then plan it from there. I don't want you coming in and being just another saloon pianist.'(PC)

It was not, therefore, until the fall of 1950 that Peterson returned to the States, consolidating his debut with a full JATP tour. Oscar believes that it was this 1950 engagement, rather than the explosive single concert, which truly launched him in America; and recorded evidence bears him out decisively. To listen to even his earliest American recordings is to be made aware of a major development from the cuts Oscar did for Canadian RCA in the late 40s. The latter feature boogie-woogie to a considerable degree, and his treatment of ballads evinces a certain naivety for all the technical accomplishment. In contrast, such Verve tracks as *Gai*, *Jumpin' With Symphony Sid* and *Exactly Like You* are the work of a mature artist. For by now Peterson was no tyro. Nurtured and stimulated by a full-scale exposure to American jazz and an intimacy with its leading practitioners, Peterson had already forged in essence the style that was to remain the fountainhead of his work henceforth. A fully-developed jazz heavyweight had arrived.

TWO

Hello Herbie:
The Guitar Trios, 1951–8

There was a love in that group that I would have to say showed in the music. (PC)

Oscar Peterson on the Brown-Ellis trio, 53–58

Peterson's first American recordings were with bassist Major Holley; but within a short while he had established a partnership with Ray Brown, who had played with him on the 1949 Carnegie Hall debut. Brown was already famous: he had been a youthful star of the magnificent Dizzy Gillespie big band, and he was also on the first recordings of the group that was to become the Modern Jazz Quartet, with the substitution of Percy Heath for Ray. Granz was anxious for his new pianist to work with the best, and Ray and Oscar hit it off at once, both musically and personally. Thus began a professional association that was to last for fifteen unbroken years.

They began as a duo, and their first working trio was with a drummer, the late Charlie Smith. (The outfit was never recorded.) Within a few months, however, Peterson had decided on a piano-guitar-bass instrumentation. Initially Barney Kessel filled the guitar slot, staying for exactly a year, and then Irving Ashby, a subtle and sadly under-recorded musician, replaced him. By 1953 Herb Ellis had taken over from Ashby, and this group stayed together for nearly six years, apart from a few months in 1955, when Kenny Burrell deputised during Ellis's illness.

This particular trio format had been made famous in the 1940s by Nat 'King' Cole; and it is no accident that Peterson's own playing at this time has a distinct Cole-ish flavour. It has been suggested that Oscar chose this instrumentation under the influence of the early 40s recordings Art Tatum made with guitarist Tiny Grimes and bassist Slam Stewart; but despite the colossal impact that Tatum had had on Oscar, the latter's recorded work is closer in style to Cole's or Hank Jones's than Tatum's. There is, even at express tempi, the same delicacy of touch, a similar way of phrasing, the mastery of dynamics, and the affinity for the blues that characterise those two splendid pianists. In addition, Cole was influenced by the now all-but-forgotten Kenny Kersey, who had worked with Irving

21

Ashby on a number of dates (notably a Coleman Hawkins-Lester Young session on Spotlite), and whose style strikes today's listener as distinctly Petersonian.

An additional connection between Cole and Peterson was Oscar's singing voice, featured on a number of early recordings and which bears an almost uncanny resemblance to Nat's. Cole was to forsake jazz piano for the world of popular singing, in which he became a performer of matchless elegance. Cynics have tended to assume that Cole changed direction in this way for financial reasons; but another possible reason presents itself in Oscar's recollection that

> Nat came in to hear me one night. He sat and listened throughout the whole evening's show and then came backstage afterwards and said, 'Look, I'll make a deal with you. You don't sing, and I won't play piano.'[1]

Certainly, Peterson did not sing on record afterwards until 1966, the year after Cole died: the album concerned was a tribute to Cole, *With Respect To Nat*.

The earlier trios with Kessel and Ashby show a greater debt to Cole's conception of the group sound than does the Ellis outfit. In his first groups Oscar's piano, like Cole's, is obviously dominant. There are occasional solos for guitarist and Brown, as there were for Oscar Moore and Wesley Prince in Nat's group; but the emphasis is on a tightly integrated and thoughtfully arranged approach that affords maximum focus on the piano. With Ellis, however, Oscar and Ray evolved a sound that is notably more ambitious and 'egalitarian'. One of the reasons for this development was the earthy fullness of Ellis's tone, which fleshed out the group's sound substantially; but a more profound explanation lies in the way the instruments worked *for* rather than merely *with* each other. Peterson remembers this group as a turning-point:

> It was the first group that really reached a depth of clarity about what we wanted to do, *and the way, not I, but the group wanted to sound*. We had three rhythmically-conscious men. We had three improvisors. Most important, we didn't have two, but *three* people that were really involved in playing for one another. I don't think just Herbie and Ray were involved in playing for me, which they did, beautifully: it was also the way Ray made *me* come up with the best possible background for Herbie. . . And the same thing would have to be said when Herbie and I played for Ray. (PC)

(My italics)

22

To listen to the various groups' recordings is indeed to become aware of this change, whereby Oscar moves from featured soloist to *primus inter pares*. Tracks with Kessell such as *C-Jam Blues, Seven Come Eleven* and the legendary *Tenderly* (all recorded on October 11, 1952) generate formidable power; but Oscar's piano is totally ascendant in arrangements meticulously conceived with his lines in mind. But recordings made less than a year later with Ellis in September 1953 document a greater sonority and considerably increased interplay. *Lollobrigida, Prompton Turnpike* and *Swingin' Till The Girls Come Home* display much more room for Ellis and Brown, not just in solo but in their *trio* lines, and achieve the status of genuine chamber jazz.

The group's repertoire rapidly became enormous. It was also highly catholic: there were originals, a rich crop of standards, bop numbers, jazz classics, show tunes, and a large number of blues. The trio's versatility and collective memory became legendary; and as Ray Brown has stressed, there was an excellent reason for such encyclopedic facility:

'We worked at it every day, every night. And if you want to be that good playing jazz, you have to work at it all the time... We did a variety of things, and Oscar wrote some hard music; but he didn't write it down. We had to memorise all of it... And Oscar would play a tune in one key one night and walk in and play the whole arrangement in another key a week later.'[2]

And Ben Webster remembers:

'I never saw anyone as keen on music as Oscar and Ray. They were always working on something or going over something to make it better. I remember being on a JATP tour with them, and at every concert, when the curtains went down for the interval, they'd be there right behind the curtain rehearsing something, right through till the concert began again. They'd be at it before the concert and after it as well.'[3]

Such dedication has its amusing side. Peterson is a fun-loving man, and no doubt such a trait has some bearing on his penchant for changing keys. When he first worked with English drummer Martin Drew (now his regular percussionist), they rehearsed a number until Drew was satisfied he had mastered the arrangement. When it came to the performance, however, Peterson led off into the tune at double the tempo they had rehearsed! A floundering Drew just managed to cope

23

without falling completely apart, to be 'rewarded' by Oscar muttering amidst the applause at the end, 'I thought you knew that arrangement.' In the same vein, Oscar has been known to tap his foot loudly at a different tempo from the one being played, just to ensure that his group is paying proper attention!

But if such moments smack somewhat of the gagster, they also reveal an absolute determination that the group's music will remain fresh through all its many engagements. Peterson's view is that if the musicians *themselves* aren't fully switched-on, there is little chance of satisfying the audience; and he is of course as stern with himself as with his confrères:

> Doing what we do demands that you have not only your senses about you, but complete interest and devotion and involvement in what you do, or else it doesn't come off. If I were to come in one night and not communicate what I should communicate to my trio, it would fall flat on its face.[4]

By 1955 Peterson's reputation was colossal. When, during a visit to England, he walked into a London jazz club, every musician in the room stiffened in awe. He had started to win all the major jazz polls, and the trio's recordings were legion, both in their own right and as Norman Granz's 'house' rhythm section. Such prolific exposure had its disadvantages. Not all of Peterson's records were top-flight jazz, for a number of studio sessions were devoted to the work of this or that songwriter, rather than reflecting the searching and broad repertoire featured on the road. In addition, familiarity began to breed contempt amongst the jazz critics: it is from this time that the canards of 'glib' and 'mechanical' start to appear in assessments of his work.

There are occasions, perhaps, when there is some justice in such remarks. But on the whole one's overriding impression is that Oscar's detractors did not listen to his work with anything like enough care. In any event, history has vindicated him. Many of his 50s dates, dismissed and derided at the time, now have the status of classics. Albums such as *Live At The Nichegei Theatre, At the Concertgebauw* and *At The Stratford Ontario Shakespeare Festival* offer a feast of varied trio jazz, and alone dispel several ill-informed myths. The range of tempi and ambience makes nonsense of the notion that Oscar is primarily a 'sweat merchant' who delights in express performances. The delicacy and rich harmonic invention of pieces like *Flamingo* and *Alone Together* repudiate the charge that Peterson was at this time a shallow and predictable interpreter of ballads; and the somewhat vicious contention voiced by Miles Davis that Oscar 'sounds as if he had to *learn* to play the blues' seems mere childish, envious drivel when one listens with proper attention to *Bluesology* or *Love You Madly*.

In sum, the Ellis outfit was distinguished for its wide sweep of material, the breadth of musical mood and texture, the precision and range of dynamics, and a joyous, earthy ferocity of pulse eloquent of the most tenacious jazz roots. And although it is invidious to attempt any judgement about which is/was Peterson's 'best' group, the Ellis trio can certainly be considered as the finest piano-bass-guitar group ever. The drive, sonority, and almost spooky level of communication are as phenomenal now as when the group were playing and recording. And although Oscar's own playing was to rise to even greater heights, I don't think he ever bettered the kind of harmonious interplay and naked swinging power that he, Ray and Herbie evolved. It was a group based on love; and that still comes across irresistibly from the records twenty-five years on.

THREE

Drums In My Ears: 1958–71

I don't think I played any harder with the drums. It's just that the two formats demand two different things. (PC)

Oscar Peterson, 1974

After six years with Peterson and Brown, Herb Ellis found he was tired, not of the music, but of the constant touring, and he left to settle in California. It was an amicable parting, but also an almost traumatic one for Oscar. He and Herbie had grown as close as brothers and his departure was a major personal wrench. But it was also a major musical one. For in the months preceding Ellis's departure, Peterson, dwelling on the question of a replacement, came to the view that he would not seek another guitarist. 'Herbie spoiled me for the rest,' he said later.

But it is posible that there was another reason. The sheer fact of Ellis's going may have led Oscar to feel that he was ready for a new challenge, an altered approach to the piano. It was not, perhaps, just the impossibility of finding another Herbie, but that Oscar felt he had achieved all he could within a guitar trio format. Accordingly, in the fall of 1958, he hired Gene Gammage, who had worked with the guitar trio from time to time, as his drummer. The new group cut one album on November 18, 1958, a jazz version of *My Fair Lady*; but Gammage's tenure was not wholly successful, and by the spring of 1959 the percussionist was Ed Thigpen, who had previously been with Billy Taylor.

Thigpen's baptism could not have been fiercer. In the summer of 1959, the trio played a four-week season at Chicago's London House, and in the day time they moved into Verve's studios and re-recorded a substantial part of the Peterson-Brown repertoire. No fewer than 124 tracks were cut in six days, and the group threw in an appearance at the Chicago *Playboy* jazz festival for good measure. Small wonder that by the end of this varied marathon Thigpen was already fitting in like a veteran.

To be candid, few of the recordings just mentioned are 'first division' Peterson. There is one superb album of Ellington songs; but in the main the performances are too short to be fully satisfying. Yet they are fascinating material for any Peterson historian, for they document a

2 The Trio in England, 1965 (Hans Harzheim)

marked change in approach from Oscar and a momentous shift in group dynamics.

It is easy to imagine that the arrival of a drummer would require not only a more percussive style from the pianist, but also a tighter, more limited harmonic approach from the group. This is not the case, however. The drum trio evinced from the start a formidable drive, but it never achieved the same naked ferocity of swing that ignites the greatest of the Ellis trio sides. That might seem odd; but in fact the new group did not *try* to match the old one in all things. In a way, of course, it *could* not do so, having replaced a harmonic instrument with a solely percussive one. As Oscar himself put it:

> Playing in a trio with a guitar, you have to be aware of what you're playing according to the harmonic clusters – you could be stepping on or contradicting the moving progressions that the guitarist is laying down for you. . . Most people then think that once you're out of a trio with a guitar and you enter one with drums, that is complete freedom. It isn't. On the contrary, you have to complement what the bass player is doing by *not* taking the place of the guitar – you can't.(PC)

These remarks illuminate several facets of the new trio's style. To begin with, they explain why Oscar's playing, while more obviously two-handed (which was to be expected), did not attempt to emulate on its own the orchestral density that guitar and piano could achieve. They also show why the group's arrangements were wider and more thoughtfully lyrical either than had been the case or than most listeners had anticipated. And above all they explain the greatly increased space afforded Ray Brown. In the guitar trios, he had been a virtuoso soloist and the group sound's absolute rock; the changed format allowed him greater fluidity, so that his lines have the kind of constant melodic creativity that is associated with the father of modern bass-playing, Jimmy Blanton. As a result, amidst the continuing high pressure of the trio's rhythmic authority, there emerged a broadened imagination and a deeper textural sophistication.

This change was, clearly, due in part to the revised format; but it was also due to the kind of material and context that characterise Oscar's records from the early 60s onwards. And *that* change has its roots in an important external event.

In 1961 Norman Granz sold Verve records to MGM for $2.8 million.

He had been looking for a buyer for some two years, having presented his last JATP tour in 1957; for while he was manager to both Oscar and Ella Fitzgerald, he was becoming less and less interested in the label the bigger it got.* More crucially, the jazz scene had changed, and to Granz's mind, changed drastically. Tatum, Parker and Young were dead; Stan Getz had temporarily emigrated to Scandinavia; Miles Davis was the new Messiah; and the onset of Ornette Coleman and Free Jazz was beckoning vigorously. So Granz got out while he was still enjoying some of his employees' work.

Verve's new owners kept Granz on in an advisory capacity for a year; but this codicil proved to be entirely notional. MGM hired Creed Taylor as the label's new executive director, and he at once embarked on a policy very different from Granz's. It was, in a word, commercial: he had been hired to make money with jazz artists, and Granz's original ideals were forgotten. Taylor's first major decision was to fire all Verve's contract artists except Johnny Hodges, Getz, Ella, and Peterson. Granz himself regarded the change as inevitable, and he is most generous about it:

> For better or worse the company stood for something when I left. But the new owners were lawyers and marketing people. I can't blame them for not caring as much as I did. It wasn't their work. And it would have been foolish of me to expect the company to have continued as before.[1]

To give Creed Taylor due credit, he served some artists well, and also sponsored a number of outstanding projects – Stan Getz and Eddie Sauter's *Focus*, important albums by gifted arrangers Gil Evans and Lalo Schifrin, and inventive technical innovations (Bill Evans's multi-tracked solo piano albums, for example). But he drowned Wes Montgomery in corn, provided the Basie orchestra with a succession of dismal dates (*Basie's Beatle Bag* was the nadir), and virtually ignored Stan Getz's outstanding quartet in favour of bossa nova and lush

---

*Verve had enjoyed several huge sellers in the late 50s, notably Ella's *Cole Porter Songbook* and a number of albums by comedians Shelly Berman and Jonathan Winters.

middle-of-the-road sessions.* Verve had always been a controversial label; but the upheaval that Taylor effected was such that before long critical reaction to the new catalogue had more than a touch of 'Come back, Norman – all is forgiven' about it.

Remarkably, amidst all this seismic change, Oscar Peterson's recording career was unaffected. Or rather, there *was* a change, but in a subtle, almost oblique way. Taylor did not involve himself personally in any Peterson session: the admirable Jim Davis produced every one, and his influence soon became apparent. For although Oscar did not in any way deviate from a true jazz path (unlike several of his less fortunate stable-mates), Davis's projects were quite distinct from the way Granz had presented Peterson on record.

Granz had showcased Oscar in three main contexts: meetings with great soloists; a large number of live recordings preserving the concert work of the trio; and studio dates devoted to the work of a particular composer. Under Davis, the 'headline' dates with other stars practically dried up, with the exception of the 1962 session with Milt Jackson. The live recordings continued, but they were club dates rather than concerts: four albums were made from the trio's 1962 engagement at the London House. But it is the studio dates which contrast most intriguingly with their 50s counterparts.

I have the highest regard for Granz; and over the thirty-five years of his close association with Oscar, there is no doubt that he has been a wise and creative influence on the pianist. But I don't think it can be denied that nearly all the 50s studio dates fail to present Peterson and his groups at their absolute best. Oscar more or less admitted this when he remarked that many people felt that 'the delicate and communicative rapport that they sensed in our in-person appearances was usually lost in the mechanical and cold confines of the studio' and that 'I am inclined to agree to the extent that our group performs much better. . . (when) a live audience is present.'[2] However, I believe that the superiority of the group's live *material* was also responsible for this disparity. The homogeneous, one composer/one artist projects did not always engage the trio's full imagination and commitment; whereas on the road, free to choose their own programmes, they responded with a total involvement

*To be fair to Taylor, the bossa nova records were so successful that it would have been absurd not to ensure their regular flow. And to be fair to Getz, the bossa nova and MOR dates all contain very fine jazz.

and the fiercer concentration that the more demanding and broader repertoire required.

What Davis encouraged Peterson to do was bring this on-the-road strength into the studio. Only one of their many sessions continued the Granz tradition of show-tune albums;* and that project, *West Side Story*, is much the most ambitious and penetrating of Peterson's outings in this genre: Oscar himself has called it 'one of the roughest projects we ever tackled', adding significantly that 'it came off differently from the other show albums.'[3] Otherwise, the sides Davis supervised used material that was both more stimulating and more jazz-focused than had largely been the case under Granz. To his great credit, Norman acknowledged this on the liner notes for *Affinity*, the trio's first session under Davis, and still among Peterson's finest albums:

'My first proposals to the trio were to play standards of the great popular composers and blues-rooted music. But now I see that Peterson has taken tunes which are not only rarely done: more than that, he has taken waltzes, which were formerly anathema to jazz, and formed them into proper jazz vehicles for his group.'

His warm essay concludes with the declaration that in this fashion Oscar has achieved 'the kind of maturity that one looks for in any kind of music but rarely finds in jazz.'

*Despite my reservations about this aspect of Granz's policy, I must admit to a great fondness for *Fiorello*, one of Norman's last dates as Oscar's producer.

Such maturity is amply documented on subsequent issues, notably the magnificent *Night Train*. This record still stands out as arguably his most ambitious, even audacious project; for, with the exception of Oscar's own beautiful *Hymn To Freedom*, the programme consists of tunes ineluctably associated with other artists. There are four classic Ellington numbers, plus tunes that seem forbiddingly soaked with the personality of their original performances – Milt Jackson's *Bags' Groove*, Hoagy Carmichael's *Georgia On My Mind*, Lester Young's *Easy Does It*. Yet Peterson surmounts all obstacles, and fashions a series of readings that are themselves classics.

Night Train was one of Oscar's biggest-selling records ever. In those days, the *Melody Maker* ran a jazz chart, and *Night Train* topped it for weeks. It was also his best received album so far by critics, featuring in several Record of the Year polls: one critic wrote 'Peterson was never a favourite pianist of mine, but this LP is quite exceptional'.[4] And to introduce a particularly personal note, *Night Train* was the first jazz record I ever bought, and was at once responsible for 'hooking' me permanently as a jazz enthusiast. An even more eloquent testament is the fact that I am currently on my fourth copy, having worn out the previous three; and I hope to live long enough to replace it several more times!

Of the other recordings made during this time, the two excellent dates with a studio big band deserve mention. Oscar fronting a large ensemble has always been an exhilarating formula; and the sessions arranged by Russell Garcia (1960) and Basie alumnus Ernie Wilkins (1962) were Oscar's first in this setting since the 1952 guest appearance with the Basie orchestra. As noted, the clutch of London House recordings continued the tradition of in-person performances; there is also a double album of the trio's Tokyo concert of 1964 (produced by Granz, and not released until the 70s, on Japanese Pablo), which offers an intriguing cross-section of material available on the studio Verves. The contrast between the two versions of *Bags' Groove* is particularly arresting: the concert performance is much faster and more extrovert than the one on *Night Train*. Both are superb in their quite separate ways, and together they testify to the range and intelligence of Peterson's pianistic imagination.

The Brown-Thigpen trio was, in its different way, as tightly integrated and as egalitarian as the Ellis group, and retained its predecessor's reputation as the finest in jazz. Thigpen emerged as one of the best small-group drummers ever. A musician first and a drummer second, he displayed not only impeccable taste and flawless swing, but also an almost *melodic* style. One of his rare extended solos is preserved on the 1962 club date, *The Sound Of The Trio*: executed entirely with brushes, *Thags' Dance* is in composer Peterson's words, 'a soft shoe shuffle' of unusual wit and variety. It is very much in keeping with this musicianly approach that a later Verve date featuring Thigpen as a leader finds him experimenting with 'singing' drums and attempting to play tunes on his kit:* only Max Roach of other leading percussionists has shown such consistent enterprise. Perhaps most fundamentally, Ed Thigpen, like Oscar and Ray, was and is steeped in the oldest, most central of jazz

*The album was *Out Of The Storm,* on Verve SVLP 9144

values. Leonard Feather has remarked that Ed is 'an encyclopedia of jazz drumming';[5] and the group's astounding range of musical vocabulary and grammar owed as much to its percussionist as it did to its founder members.

The mid-60s was a time of considerable ferment for Peterson. He remarried; he left Verve in 1964;† and, most important of all, he lost in rapid succession the services of Ed Thigpen and Ray Brown.

Thigpen had been in the group for as long as Herb Ellis, and his decision to quit the road and settle in Toronto was itself a big blow. But a few months later Ray Brown announced that he too had had enough of touring – Ray Brown, the man who had been Oscar's left hand and intimate friend for fifteen years. ('That's longer,' Brown said later in simulated awe, 'than most guys stay with their wives!'[6]) The parting was entirely amicable, naturally enough. Oscar and Ray had achieved great things as performers, and they had also, along with Thigpen, founded the Advanced School of Contemporary Music in Toronto. Brown himself has stressed that his departure was occasioned by fatigue and a long-term concern for his health:

> 'Some of those tours were really punishing – we'd come to Europe and do 62 one-nighters in 65 days – and then I started to think, "Hey! I don't need this much money!"... I think Oscar and I built something between us that will always stand up musically. It was just that one day I looked up and realised that I'd turned 40, and although the money was great the tour schedules were heavy. So I decided to quit.'[7]

Oscar was later to say, 'You can't *replace* Ray Brown – it's not possible';[8] but he found himself a notably gifted bass player soon enough – Sam Jones. Like Louis Hayes, who had taken over the drum chair from Ed Thigpen a few months before, Jones had been working for years with Cannonball Adderley, whose musical values and articulate intelligence were close to Peterson's own;* so it was no surprise that when Oscar took his new group on the road after several months of rehearsal, it was a great success.

†The *We Get Requests* album of that year signposts this departure with a valediction to producer Jim Davis, the Peterson original *Goodbye J.D.*

*Given this affinity, it is remarkable that Adderley and Peterson never recorded together – the more so when one remembers that Oscar worked with virtually all the major players in the modern/mainstream bracket.

35

3 The Trio: Ray Brown and Ed Thigpen (Hans Harzheim)

Uniquely in Peterson's career, the records made by this trio do not do it justice. In 1964 Oscar had signed to Mercury, and most of his records came out on the short-lived Limelight label, Mercury's jazz subsidiary. An auspicious start was made with *Oscar Peterson + One*, a Brown-Thigpen date that added the sparkling trumpet and flugelhorn of Clark Terry; and the old trio also cut *Canadiana Suite*, which I discuss in Chapter Six. But *Blues Etude*, Jones's and Hayes's debut with Oscar can hardly be counted among Peterson's finest sessions. It is historically interesting, in that one side has Hayes and Brown while the other showcases the new group; but although the music is immaculate, it pales when set beside many albums from previous groups. And *Soul Espagnol* and *With Respect to Nat*, while agreeable, belong as much to the 'easy listening' category as to bona fide jazz. When one compares these pleasant but unremarkable records to the 1966 concerts the group gave in England, it seems a great shame that such slaughtering (and much more representative) performances were not taped. As it is, we had to wait for the group's Pablo reunion in the 1970s to hear them produce on record the calibre of jazz they achieved on the road.

Oscar left Mercury after only three and a half years; and this paved the way for the release of some of the most remarkable recordings in jazz history. Since the early 60s Oscar had been making annual visits to the Black Forest home of Hans Georg Brunner-Schwer, and giving private concerts to fellow guests. Brunner-Schwer, boss of MPS records, is an outstanding recording engineer, and his home included what amounted to a full-scale studio. Accordingly, he taped a good deal of the music Peterson played, although at the time there was no thought of them being anything other than private recordings. However, when Peterson's contractural obligations to other companies terminated in 1968, he and Brunner-Schwer agreed to the commercial release of a number of albums.

The first six were issued severally under the generic title of *Exclusively For My Friends*, and another nine Peterson albums on MPS were to follow. The first thing to stress about them is the quality of the sound reproduction, which set new standards for all recording. When I bought the first issued of these albums, *The Way I Really Play*, it was a major (though wonderful) shock to hear Oscar's sound captured with full accuracy on record for the first time. Nor was I the only one to be thus impressed. A host of critics whose response to Peterson had been hitherto lukewarm at most climbed all over themselves to pronounce their admiration for the album. One, a reviewer in *Jazz Monthly*, was so struck by the splendour of a pianist he had always deemed 'shallow' that he argued that it should be retitled *The Way I* Rarely *Play*. In fact, no discernible change, either in style or achievement, informs the music itself: it is more, perhaps, that the audio fidelity enabled certain listeners to appreciate the subtlety and authority of Oscar's playing for the first time.

The records preserve performances by all Peterson's groups from the Thigpen-Brown outfit onwards, although unfortunately only one track features the Jones-Hayes trio indifferently served by Mercury. The overall standard is exceptionally high, and includes the momentous *My Favourite Instrument*, Oscar's first solo album, of which more later.

In the meantime, Louis Hayes had left the group in 1967 to strike out on his own as a leader, and was replaced by Bobby Durham, who joined Oscar from Duke Ellington's orchestra. Announcing this on a 1969 tour of England, Oscar quipped, 'That's kind of heavy, huh? Stealing from Duke is like stealing from the Royal Bank of Canada!' Durham stayed with Peterson until the early 70s, when Oscar temporarily disbanded and embarked on a solo career. He is an able percussionist in the Thigpen mould; but it is with this trio that signs of change in Oscar's own playing, and in his conception of the group, began to emerge.

I've stressed that Peterson's trios from 1953 onwards were distinguished for their integration and three-way interplay. The Jones-Durham trio, however, seem not to have made this its major goal. It quickly became the *tightest* group Peterson has ever had; but Oscar's approach established him as more obviously the leader and featured soloist than at any time since the days with Kessell and Ashby. His own tribute to his rhythm section both sums up their qualities *and* the implicit shift from a set-up where Oscar had been *primus inter pares*: 'Sam Jones and Bobby Durham let themselves be caught up by the piano, and I can trust them blindly.'[9] This is not to say that this trio was Oscar plus *merely* rhythm accompaniment: no Peterson group has been that. But it is significant that Jones very rarely solos, and that the group's style is centred on the piano in a much more closely focused way than characterised the Brown-Thigpen trio. Tracks such as the majestic *Satin Doll*, *Down Here On The Ground*, and *Sax No End* are supreme bravura piano jazz given the best possible underpinning by an expert rhythm section; but their conception is distinct from the approach that Peterson had embraced before, or was indeed to return to.

4 A 1953 study of Oscar with Ray and Herbie (Melody
Maker)

It is legitimate to infer from this movement towards a piano-centred trio the germination of Oscar's desire to play solo piano as well. *My Favourite Instrument* and a second solo programme for MPS, *Tracks*, showed that Peterson was uniquely equipped in the genre. On his own he was able to explore the possibilites of a tune more freely than is ever possible in a group; and the moving and richly penetrating readings of *Django, Dancing On The Ceiling, Little Girl Blue* and *I Should Care* display an astonishing fleetness and depth of imagination. In a different vein, the joyous *Perdido, A Little Jazz Exercise* (quite an understatement!) and *Honeysuckle Rose* demonstrate that Oscar's extrovert authority and inimitable swing are not at all diminished by the absence of a rhythm section. Moreover, such performances find him taking triumphant rhythmic risks that none but the most insensitively egoistical *group* pianist would think of indulging.

However, superb though these two albums are, there can be little doubt that this imminent new peak in Peterson's career was accelerated and enriched by an external event – Norman Granz's return to the recording business. For the creation of Pablo Records Inc. overlapped with Oscar's solo departure, and it was to ensure that the next few years would witness Oscar's greatest achievements yet.

FOUR

Solo and Pablo:
The Compleat Pianist

The first time I had to walk out on my own, I almost panicked, because just ahead of me was a well-known musical group, a quintet, and I said to myself, 'My God! There's no way – I must have my group!' (PC)

Oscar Peterson on his solo debut

I have just suggested that Peterson's departure into a solo career was telegraphed both by the solo albums he made for MPS and the change of focus evident in his recent trio work. But it must be stressed that, at the time, the move was not only audacious but required careful planning and a subtle but fundamental adjustment on Oscar's part.

The casual student of Peterson's work might assume that the switch to solo piano would be no big deal for someone so supremely accomplished. But Oscar has pointed out that this is not the case – it is not a matter of technique *as such*, but of ingrained habits and thereby of mental approach:

Sometimes, pianists, without even knowing it, start playing solo piano. They may take a chorus by themselves, or a bridge, and they enjoy it; but mentally they're not really prepared for it, for a continuance of it. When they're faced with it when suddenly someone calls them for an engagement and says 'We want you to play solo', the pianist will back off without thinking and say, 'I haven't been doing that, you know. I can't: there's no way I can come up with that'. And basically he's been doing it all the while, but he's not mentally conditioned to it. (PC)

The notion that reluctance to play solo piano is essentially a mental rather than a pianistic hang-up is further explored in these remarks about the difficulty in adjusting from a *group* approach:

In a group, a pianist can be quietly brainwashed into using less and less of his left hand – especially if he has a guitarist, because *he'll* start saying, 'You're getting in my way – don't play that much with your

43

left hand.' So he withdraws that left hand, and before you know it, if he suddenly gets a solo job, he'll be lost. It's not that he *can't* do it: it's that he's forgotten how to, he isn't used to it. (AP)

Nevertheless, Peterson's desire to launch out into this genre was clearly formidable; in addition, both Duke Ellington and Norman Granz had been urging him to take the step for some time. Accordingly, Oscar made his solo debut at the Newport Jazz Festival of 1972, playing a concert in nearby Carnegie Hall. It was a triumph; and Peterson then did a highly acclaimed season at the El Matador club in San Francisco. And there is no doubt that solo playing gave him the opportunity to express himself more freely, for he had found that in recent years there had increasingly been times

when I wanted to go melodically or harmonically or rhythmically another way – just for two bars, or four. But you can't possibly transmit that kind of thing that quickly to a group. In a group, you play with a sense of a pact that you're going to do a tune in a particular way, within certain confines. If you suddenly decide to take a left turn down a one-way street, it becomes a little hazardous for the group! And what you end up with is dishevelment. (AP)

Then there is the question of a solo pianist's repertoire. The Peterson trios' library had been vast; but that was almost irrelevant when it came to playing on his own. It is interesting to note that there are many magnificent Peterson solos on group performances which he has never attempted to restructure for solo use; conversely, he has played several tunes alone which never featured in any of his trios' recordings. Naturally, there are many others which have been used in both contexts; but a full break-down would confirm that the approach to solo piano is radically different. In a 1975 interview, Peterson revealed that he was still working on establishing a repertoire, and stressed that he could only perform tunes he really wanted to play, whereas in a group he could always go along with a few unsympathetic numbers if others were keen on them. He also emphasised that he is careful to make his programme as broad as possible:

I have to be very careful about the tunes I choose. If I were to play a full set of jazz tunes, I'd have to devise a different approach because of the linear melodic content of the tunes. I don't want to go back to the be-bop piano era, where everything is linear. I don't want to do that at all.[1]

In short, Peterson's conception of solo playing was one of *total piano*. He considered it essential to evolve a style and repertoire that were genuinely orchestral – harmonically rich enough to sustain interest across a whole set, and sufficiently illustrative of what he has called 'the tremendous storehouse of musical capability that lies behind any jazz pianist.' (AP)

There are other problems about playing solo. The most obvious is the question of whether one can *swing* without rhythmic support; and jazz is fairly well-stocked with good robust pianists who do, or would, struggle under such circumstances. Equally, there are others who comfortably surmount such an obstacle – or, more positively, for whom it is no obstacle at all: Earl Hines, Count Basie, Dave McKenna, Ray Bryant, Cedar Walton and, surprisingly perhaps, Bill Evans belong to such an elite. The question is not really one of the 'disappearing left hand' that several critics have diagnosed – not *technically*, anyway. It's more a matter of emphasis and habit than basic capability. Even to an execrable amateur pianist like myself, it is obvious that one uses the left hand in a different way when playing solo from when playng in a trio. If in the former context one simply comps,* as one can do quite satisfactorily when backed up by a proficient bass, the resultant sound is going to be excessively top-register, if not tinny. Conversely, a piano virtuoso must tailor his style in a group to make maximum use of the other instruments. Simply to play as if there were no difference between a trio and a solo performance is a waste of the other musicians.†

It can readily be seen, then, that Oscar's preparation for a full-scale solo career had to be extensive. Nevertheless, as befits such a professional, the various complexities and problems had been absorbed and transcended by the time he have his first public performance; and an exhilarated jazz public waited for the recorded documentation of this latest Peterson facet. That they did not have to wait long was mainly due to Norman Granz's coincidental decision to resume recording.

*To 'comp' is to punctuate the right hand lines, or the work of another soloist, with left-hand chords. Comping is a basic method of 'feeding', but has no real flow or melodic status.
†Such profligacy, I find, mars the group work of those great pianists Errol Garner, whose two-fisted power simply drowned his rhythm section, and Art Tatum, whose law-unto-itself imagination made any genuine group interplay simply impossible.

45

It is worth going briefly into *why* Granz made such a return, for his decision was much more surprising than Oscar's venture. After all, Peterson had been moving towards such a departure, albeit 'invisibly', for some time; but Granz had given no-one the impression that he was itching to be back as a record producer. Quite the reverse: as late as 1971 he was telling Leonard Feather:

It's a disgrace what the jazz artists of today are being forced to do, recording material that is all wrong for them. It's criminal, too, that someone like Sarah Vaughan was allowed to go without making a single record for five years. And it's an outrage that of the twenty-seven albums I produced with Art Tatum, not a single one is available . . .

The record companies have changed. Executives today are only concerned with the fact that they can gross $9 million with the Rolling Stones. They forget that a profit is still a profit, that you're still making money if you only net $9 thousand. I keep telling people that, and they think I'm crazy.[2]

Such jaundiced aggressiveness hardly connotes a burning desire to be back in the fold. And yet within two years of that interview, Granz had launched Pablo Records, and at the time of writing he still seems as enthusiastic as at the start about keeping it going. What changed his mind?

One can, I think, infer from the above remarks a growing awareness amidst the surface disenchantment that the artists he most admired would go on being scandalously by-passed unless *he* did something about it. It is surely no accident, for instance, that Sarah Vaughan, whose neglect Granz so rightly fumed about, has cut at least eight albums for Pablo, restoring her to her proper pinnacle. It is no less significant that Dizzy Gillespie, whose pre-Pablo career was direly languishing under a succession of mediocre-to-awful sessions that reached an all-time low with the aptly named *Souled Out*, was at once rejuvenated by Norman's policy, and proceeded to make a string of albums that rank with the finest of his career. And it is as a direct result of Granz's patronage that Ray Bryant, Tommy Flanagan, Jimmy Rowles, Joe Turner and Benny Carter were re-established as the marvellous artists they are and had always been. In any event, whatever the private reasons for Granz's return, the fact remains that within a year of Pablo's launching, nearly all the ills that he and others of like persuasion had diagnosed were on the mend. The music he had sponsored so creatively in the 1950s once more had a regular fruitful outlet. And arguably the biggest beneficiary of all was Oscar Peterson himself.

Granz took proper account of Peterson's solo career from the beginning; but he was also clearly anxious to present Oscar in as many contexts as possible. From very early on in Pablo's catalogue it was evident that Granz wished both to recapture and if possible improve upon the ethos of the 1950s Verve dates; and although Oscar wasn't the only 'house pianist' – there was plenty of work for Flanagan, Bryant and Rowles as well – he figured widely in Pablo's projects.

I deal with the larger sessions re-uniting Oscar with such musicians as Dizzy, Milt Jackson, Roy Eldridge and Clark Terry in the next chapter. Concerning the other Pablo dates, it is evident that Granz's enterprise significantly coloured Oscar's solo career, making it an extra dimension rather than a complete departure. Oscar continued to give many solo concerts; but he also made frequent public appearances in the company of Joe Pass or bassist Niels-Henning Orsted Pedersen, or both. In effect, we began to be treated to several Oscars at once.

It is unfortunately not possible in a book of this length to offer detailed analysis of the many outstanding albums Oscar made during this period. But a few must at least be mentioned, if only because they form the apex of his recorded achievement. Indeed, the two double albums *A Salle Pleyel* and *In Russia* are so magnificent that had Oscar never recorded anything before or since, his place in jazz piano's Hall of Fame would still be assured. The Salle Pleyel concert (in March 1975) marks the first appearance on record of a regular feature of Oscar's solo concerts – the Ellington medley, with *A Train* done as a graceful waltz and a first raunchy and finally delicate *Things Ain't What They Used To Be* particularly felicitous. There is a rich exploration of *Tenderly* that is as far removed as is reasonable to imagine from the classic 1952 Brown-Kessel performance, and yet unmistakeably Petersonian. And the final solo number, *Sweet Georgia Brown*, is a performance of stupefying grandeur.* Elsewhere on the album there are seven exquisite solo performances by Joe Pass, and then six duets. These are genuine dual improvisations: while sharply aware of each other's lines and sympathetically complementary, their playing constantly filigrees and re-

*A detailed analysis of this track can be found in Part Three.

47

colours each separate idea. The authority that Peterson had developed as a solo performer is fed back into his encounters with others in the form of an even greater sophistication and audacity of imagination. In addition, both men swing so virulently that it is easy to fool oneself into hearing a ghost drummer at times!

In Russia commemorates a short tour that Oscar undertook in 1974, in the company of NHOP and ex-Woody Herman drummer Jake Hanna. In most respects the tour was not a great success: indeed, it was cut short. Peterson has always been guarded in his public statements about why this happened; but it seems reasonably clear that the trio was subjected to a good deal of hassle and policing, and eventually got fed up with it and cancelled out. Musically, however, at least on the evidence of the record, it was triumphant. This is not just because the three play so well: to a Western listener, the hipness of Oscar's audience is a delightful revelation. Their knowledge of his repertoire seems legion – recognitory applause instantly greets most of the numbers – and their enthusiastic empathy even extends to off-beat claps during the bluesy coda to *Hallelujah Time*. Maybe it was this hipness that occasioned the trio's subsequent trouble: in a land where jazz is officially 'decadent' and records supposed to be illegal despite a flourishing black market, Party bosses can't have been any too thrilled to find Peterson's work so intimately known by the Russian people!

It is the solo moments that impress most on this album, including the stunning boogie-woogie on *Hallelujah Time* and a near-incredible passage in the trio's *Just Friends*, where at a speed in excess of 90 bars-a-minute Oscar produces the most delicate of melodic improvisations over an irresistible and lightly-touched stride foundation. But the developing empathy with bassist Pedersen is also a major delight, and leads me to an important and fascinating point.

One aspect of Peterson's career, and indeed of the authority of his musical personality, that has often been taken for granted is his long-term partnership with two of the very best bassists in jazz history. The fifteen years with Ray Brown has eventually been succeeded by an association with Neils-Henning Orsted Pedersen that is already over a decade old and still flourishing mightily. Cynics might imagine that the bassists' chief motivation was and is money; but consigning that to the critical compost heap where it belongs, it is not only clear that such longevity is eloquent of the satisfaction of playing with Oscar, but also most instructive to consider the separate and profound effect each bass virtuoso has had on Peterson himself. As a local attempt to define each bassist's style and influence, I'd like to look briefly at two versions of the tune Ray introduced into the Peterson repertoire in the early 1960s – *You Look Good To Me*.

The 1964 version* is a testament to Gunther Schuller's insight into Ray's matchless ability to 'drive a unit of any size' through the sheer length and impetus of his notes. Schuller deftly defines the elusive concept of 'swinging' as happening when 'the rhythm mass moves in a horizontal direction and is not merely a vertical coincidence of things happening together', and concludes that Ray will always swing any performance because he never fails to effect 'this horizontal movement because his notes are so long and because his tone projects a feeling of moving forward all the time'.[3] Such characteristics are indeed the driving force of this first cut of *You Look Good To Me*. He fleshes out the elementary chord sequence in his early solo; and his singing lines at the root of the tune's development allow Oscar to adopt a positively laid-back approach, his delicate right hand exposition articulated fractionally behind Ray's surging notes, creating a formidable sense of swinging untapped power. At no time does Peterson play louder than *mezzoforte*, even at the climax; and yet the performance sizzles with the kind of effortless virility that Ray and Oscar could always produce.

The 1981 cut* is quite different. For a start there is a strong impression that Oscar is utterly familiar with the tune, having played it God knows how many times in the interim. But while such intimacy might explain in part the greater pace and attack of the performance, that is only a superficial consideration. This interpretation is radically altered by NHOP's different style. Whereas Brown's lines, for all their fullness and energizing size, are pizzicato throughout, Pedersen's playing describes an india-rubber, serpentine legato. His separate notes are completely distinct; and yet they flow into each other with an unbroken suppleness that quite transforms the overall group sound. As a result, it is *Oscar* this time who pushes ahead of the beat, not the bassist, effecting a tension equal in excitement to the earlier trio's but also separate from it. Peterson's playing is quite simply much *louder*, too – especially at the climax, where a descending figure is articulated

*On *We Get Requests* with Brown and Ed Thigpen, Verve SVLP 9086.

*On *Nigerian Marketplace* with Pedersen and drummer Terry Clark, Pablo D2308 231.

fortissimo in order to balance NHOP's lines that surge through like a flood tide. Of course, there is nothing estimable in itself about playing either loudly or softly; but it is intriguing that the more delicate of these performances date from a time when Peterson was still being pilloried for over-use of technique and for a self-indulgent, bullying style. Together the two versions of *You Look Good To Me* demonstrate two things: that Peterson's sensitiveness to the musicians around him has always been finely-honed and highly responsive in terms of the effects of his own style; and that his excursions into solo piano subtly translated his approach to group dynamics, structure and improvisation.

I end this chapter with a consideration of the three albums collected under the titles *The History Of An Artist* (a double album) and *The History Of An Artist Vol 2*. For this project, Oscar and Norman Granz conceived the idea of re-creating all the stages of Peterson's career from his U.S. debut onwards – the duo with Brown, the various guitar trios, the drum groups, and the solo performances. Accordingly, nearly all Oscar's past colleagues are re-united with him: the only one absent is Ed Thigpen, who by this time (December 1972) had emigrated to Scandinavia. But Irving Ashby is on the date, and he responds splendidly to the opportunity to record again at last, notably on the majestic blues *This Is Where It's At*.

The interim revolution in recording techniques makes comparative listening tricky; but although the duo tracks with Brown are noticeably more full-bodied in sound, they relate very closely to the 1950 performances that chronicle Oscar's first Verve cuts. The piano is perhaps more expansive; but one should expect no less from an artist of 48 as opposed to his counterpart of 25. The real point here, as throughout the albums, is that the music is equally riveting as historical pastiche *and* a performance in its own right. It is fascinating, for example, to hear how the progressive Georg Mraz on bass* alters the balance and approach of the group relative to the re-created sides with Sam Jones. *Richard's Round* is a waspishly urgent tune that the trio tear into virulently, and Peterson's lines are more savage and oblique, amidst the swinging euphoria, than one is accustomed to hearing from him when with more conservative colleagues.

*Mraz was part of Oscar's trio in 1970, and is on two MPS dates.

One major characteristic that the albums endorse is the feeling that Oscar never swung more ferociously than in the early guitar trios. Two of the tracks with Kessel, *Wes's Tune* and the delicious *Ma, He's Making Eyes At Me*, and *I Want To Be Happy* with Ellis are jet-propelled in their force, Brown's huge notes setting up a naked drive that none of the drum trios ever quite matched. And the solo track, *Lady Of The Lavender Mist*, is a gorgeous expression of Peterson's reflective maturity. This lovely snippet of Ellingtonia is so neglected a tune that Duke himself once asked Oscar, 'Who wrote that last song you played?'! Peterson has since featured the tune many times; but I've never heard him play it better than on this record. Its tender romanticism and rhythmic subtlety are a noble testament to the genius of both men.

For the Peterson student, and indeed any serious jazz historian, *The History Of An Artist* is arguably Oscar's most important record. The reconstruction of the various aspects of his career and the subtle shifts in his style not only work triumphantly as living jazz of the 1970s, but also vindicate and illuminate all those past performances.

Pablo is still flourishing; and it is to be supposed that the label will continue to feature Oscar both as a soloist and as the lynch-pin of further invigorating ensembles and 'matches'. It is to be hoped, too, that Granz will see his way to recording Peterson as a solo player to the extent he afforded Art Tatum with the *Solo Masterpieces* project. But even if not another note is preserved for posterity, Oscar Peterson's Pablo recordings are guaranteed long-lived fame, as central to the ethos and achievement of jazz piano as Bud Powell's Verves and Blue Notes, Waller's RCA's, Bill Evans's Riversides, Monk's Blue Notes, and of course Tatum's albums for Granz. They coincide with his absolute flowering as a performer, a jazz pianist at home in all contexts and capable of igniting any session. Whether playing in the familar settings of trio or solo, or in such unusual projects as the 'Satch and Josh' duets with Basie, the *Porgy and Bess* with Joe Pass where Oscar plays clavichord, or on the several albums when the Belgian harmonica player Toots Thielemans is added, Peterson on record and in concert has emerged as the Compleat Pianist. There seems to be little that he hasn't done and even less that he can't do.

FIVE

Just You, Just Me:
Peterson as Accompanist

The best accompanying pianist I ever had was Oscar Peterson. He listens to the hornmen and seems to know exactly what they're going to play, and sets it up for them instinctively. [1]

Ben Webster

Early on in Peterson's career, Granz began to use him as his 'house pianist'. Initially this simply meant that Oscar and the trio served as the rhythm section on JATP tours. But soon Granz set up specific studio dates with a variety of artists, and in at least seven cases out of ten he chose Peterson as the backing pianist.

On the face of it, such a choice was neither obvious nor wise. Peterson was young and still inexperienced, despite his recent saturation in the U.S. jazz scene. Moreover, he was such a powerful soloist that one might doubt if he possessed the necessary restraint to place himself in the background. After all, his idol Art Tatum had proved to be a hopelessly bullying accompanist. That is not to say that Tatum made no good records in others' company: on the contrary, his meetings with Hampton, Webster and Carter remain classics to this day. But in each case Tatum is co-protagonist rather than accompanist; and it would not have been unreasonable to expect Oscar's efforts to be of a similar mould.

Nothing could be further from the truth. On scores of dates Oscar proved himself an accompanist of uncommon sensitivity and exceptional intelligence, capable of adjusting his style (at times radically) to the particular needs of each musician. His training as a classical pianist was doubtless a major benefit in this field; even more crucial was the fact that he has always been an avid and astute listener to music of all kinds. And when he spoke to Steve Voce in 1971 about the various dates, his comments were notable for the acuteness of his musical awareness:

> I'm very fond of accompanying other soloists. Ben Webster, for instance. It's always a shining hour for us to make an album with

Ben. Dizzy, Charlie Parker, Lester Young– it was always marvellous to work with such great players. I've had the pleasure of accompanying Billie on several albums, but I must say my utmost favourite was Ella– it's such a joy to play for Ella. But then there are so many: Stan Getz was a gas.

The interesting thing is that people see you playing for different soloists and they take it for granted that, well, if you can play for one, you can play for them all. But as you can realise, they all approach their solo thing differently. Stan likes a lush, percussive cushion underneath him. Dizzy loves fire, utter fire at all times. Ben likes flow, he likes a harmonic flow. It's a challenge to play accompaniments for these great artists.[2]

And as he told Peter Clayton a few years later, 'I can honestly say that I can't think of one of those sessions– whether it be Ben, Sonny Stitt, Roy Eldridge– that wasn't exciting'. (PC) Exciting to hear they undoubtedly are; but the excitement Oscar felt derives from a scholarly reverence for those artists' roots and contribution to jazz, plus an enormous affection for them: the sessions are eloquent of a lot of love.

It is never easy to nibble when one wants to gorge oneself; but considerations of space mean that I can only offer a quick tour of some of the most notable records that make up such a cornucopia. *The Parker Jam Session* (July 1952) is alone memorable for the presence of the three most important altoists in jazz's genesis (up to Ornette Coleman, of course) – Parker, Hodges and Carter. To hear this triumvirate in successive choruses of the date's two blues is to receive a profound lesson, not only in the roots and grammar of jazz, but in how superficial are the demarcations that jazz theorists propose when talking of 'schools' or 'eras'. Parker's rhythmic sense is unquestionably more 'advanced' than his two colleagues; but they're all coming through the same door. And Oscar's playing is wonderfully apposite throughout: it is especially satisfying to witness the different lines he sets down for Parker, being instantly alive to his different needs.

No less successful is the 1957 Chicago Opera House concert starring Stan Getz and J.J. Johnson. Peterson does not even solo; but his background is perfect for both hornmen, and they play as well as at any time in their distinguished careers. Getz's ballad feature, *It Never Entered My Mind*, is still one of his greatest performances, and owes much to Oscar's delicate, unobtrusive harmonic cushion. In a quite different context, Peterson's style with the attacking Lionel Hampton greatly impresses also. The *Jazz Ambassadors* sessions (with Brown and Buddy Rich) find Hampton, as always, leading from the front: Oscar, quite unlike Tatum when he worked with Hampton, stays sympathetically out of the way, concentrating on laying down the kind of floating base that inspires Hampton's most creative flights. Even in solo Oscar keeps himself somewhat in check, anxious to create a contrast with Hampton's extrovert soaring and thus balance it. And as an example of how to *push* a 'hot' soloist rather than unobtrusively letting him burn, *Birks* from a 1955 Stockholm JATP date could not be bettered. During Roy Eldridge's solo, the rhythm section was, in Granz's pungent words, 'right up Roy's ass': a happily goaded Roy nearly takes the paint off the wall in response. Urged on by Brown at his most majestic and Oscar's simple but ballsy riffs, Roy's muted trumpet outing is the single most exciting solo I know, and it is almost shocking to think that at this time many regarded him as a mere hang-over from the past, unfashionable and irrelevant in an era dominated by Miles Davies and Chet Baker.

It would not be true to suggest that *all* Peterson's companions invariably produced their best work with him. Good though his cuts with Billie Holiday are, those she made with Teddy Wilson or Jimmy Rowles are superior. Wilson, again, and Nat Cole also seem to have been better for the declining Lester Young, although I must say that I find critical dismissal of the Young-Peterson tracks very much overstated. Peterson in solo here is more voluble than Cole, and the contrast with Lester's lazy, spare power might seem to disrupt the performances as a whole; but Young plays extremely well nevertheless, and his solos on *Just You, Just Me* can be counted amongst his finest later work. And, strangely, Oscar is not ideal for Coleman Hawkins on his own, despite the magnificence of his contribution to the Hawkins-Webster classic, *Blue Saxophones*. When Hawkins was ailing towards the end of his life, Oscar was a stalwart and loving accompanist for him; but in his prime he seems, on recorded evidence, to have been better served by Tommy Flanagan or Hank Jones.

Nevertheless, none of these sessions is remotely a failure or a bad mismatch; and in his work with Webster, Getz, Dizzy, Eldridge, Ella, and Stitt, Oscar inspires his associates to perfection. It is in my view impossible to find a Webster record that tops his various meetings with Peterson; and Stitt's 1959 meeting with the new Peterson trio with Thigpen remains his finest record, matchless for both his alto and tenor outings.

As noted, once Granz had sold Verve, Peterson's opportunities to shine as an accompanist were drastically reduced; but the one 'meeting date' Jim Davis organised initiated a playing relationship that was to become one of Oscar's richest – that with vibist Milt Jackson. The 1962 *Very Tall* surprised annotator Nat Hentoff into confessing that he now saw that Oscar was 'capable of underplaying, of implying a huge reserve of strength rather than going for broke in each solo'. This is an excellent summary of Oscar's thoughtful work on the album, although one does rather wonder as to how much of Peterson's previous work Hentoff was truly familiar with. The rapport is particularly close on *Work Song* and *Reunion Blues*, and the record underlines Oscar's modernism – a central characteristic that some commentators have refused to accept, placing him in the pre-bop, Tatumesque school instead. Even one spin of this album makes that latter view untenable.

Moving forward to Peterson's larger Pablo sessions, one finds that dates with Jackson feature regularly. By 1975 Jackson had finally left the MJQ, causing its dissolution; and for all that group's major achievements, Jackson's subsequent work suggests that he both needed and revelled in his new freedom. He was widely agreed to have been the star of the 1975 Montreux Festival, from which Granz released seven albums; and his headline date, teaming him with Oscar, NHOP and Mickey Roker is awesome. Milt is so good that he relegates an in-form Peterson to second place, which lies within very few musicians' compass; even so, Peterson's solo on *Night Mist* is exceptional, as is his work behind Jackson's own superlative exploration. Recently, *Ain't But A Few Of Us Left* (with Ray Brown and drummer Grady Tate) and *Two Of The Few*, a programme of duets, have maintained and extended this most fruitful of partnerships.

A musician on whom Oscar has had a recent galvanising effect, and with whom he had never worked before, is trumpeter Freddie Hubbard. Freddie had begun his career as a highly imaginative and superbly equipped hard bop player. Rightly hailed as the best of the post-Davis trumpeters, he had then gone on to make a host of fusion dates that were most lucrative but aesthetically puny when set beside his earlier work and promise. No-one was more aware of this than Hubbard himself, and on a momentous occasion said as much to Norman Granz:

> We ran into each other at a jazz festival in England, and Freddie told me how badly he wanted to record with Oscar Peterson. 'To get

back', as he put it, 'to playing some real jazz, and not this shit I'm into now.'[3]

Accordingly, Granz set up several sessions for Freddie to fulfil this ambition. Two teamed him with Gillespie and Clark Terry as well, in the kind of jam session Granz has always excelled at sponsoring. The third was a headline Freddie and Oscar date, *Face To Face*. Both men are in wonderful form; and it is fascinating to hear how Peterson instinctively adapts to the idiom of hard bop, notably on Hubbard's tune *Thermo*. Peterson grew up during the original bop revolution, and his playing evinced from the beginning a vital awareness of the changes Bud Powell and the young George Shearing effected. And if hard bop, its successor, is not the first style one might associate with him, he is steeped in its grammar and values, if only by osmosis.

No discussion of Pablo or of Oscar could be complete without reference to the mighty 'Trumpet Kings' project. This most audacious of Granz's enterprises consists of five albums* that pit Oscar succes- sively against Roy Eldridge, Dizzy Gillespie, Harry Edison, Clark Terry, and Jon Faddis. And I use the preposition 'against' advisedly. The albums shine with love; but Oscar revealed that they had a competitive edge as well:

> With Diz, and Roy, and others too, there's always been a kind of gunfighter thing – you know, 'I'm going to run you out of town' sort of approach. And not just among themselves, either – it doesn't matter what instrument you play. Just before the session with Dizzy, I said to him, 'I'm going to waste you today, Birks,' which got him going – it gets us all going. Of course, it's fun; but in a way it's serious as well.[4]

Whatever the motivation and the preliminaries, the duets between Oscar and Dizzy are sensationally good, with Gillespie in the kind of form that one can only call frightening. The performance of *Caravan* is perhaps the most distinguished, its vast power and melodic invention sustained through six minutes, at a tempo that would reduce most musicians to tears of frustration. The album won the Record of the Year slot in the *Downbeat* International Critics Poll of 1976 – the first time

*There is also an extra album that collects the 'remainders' on Pablo 2310 817. No fall-off in quality should be inferred from the fact that the cuts were not included on the original releases.

that Oscar had got a '1st' in any denomination of that periodical's critics' selections. Better late than never; and it certainly could not have happened to a better record.

The other four albums are only marginally inferior, and Oscar has said that the Eldridge was for him the most moving, chiefly because of the love he has for Roy as a man and as a daring musician who puts himself on the line every time. Good though the album is – and it is additionally interesting in that Oscar plays organ on several tracks – I still feel that it is the Gillespie that shines most brightly. But the entire series is distinguished for its bravery and encyclopedic jazz mastery; and if it is ever possible, it would be good to hear it extended through meetings with Hubbard and Wynton Marsalis.

As long as there is any catholicity in jazz, Oscar Peterson will continue to be a favourite accompanist. Capable of withdrawing into the background and creating an unselfishly apposite cushion for jazzmen of virtually all persuasions, he is also a tremendous catalyst, equally capable of igniting a jaded or over-cautious player into new realms of creativity. And it is worth remembering that his name and status helped to promote a number of sessions that might otherwise have sunk without trace, or indeed not happened at all. (Witness the marvellous 1957 date with the then all-but-forgotten violinist, the matchless Stuff Smith.) When one considers the renascence of musicians like Eldridge, the Peterson dates Sonny Stitt made, the majestic latterday work of Jackson, and the Pablo-fed resurgence of Gillespie, Sarah Vaughan and the previously almost-unknown Joe Pass, even the most curmudgeonly Peterson detractor would have to acknowledge that the history of jazz wuld have been very different, and much the poorer, without the sessions that he was so delighted and proud to be on.

SIX

Hymn To Freedom:
A Note on Peterson the Composer

I am the world's laziest writer. (PC)

Oscar Peterson, 1974

There are two ways in which a jazz composer is evaluated. One is to discern how many *other* musicians use his compositions, and how productive the material proves; the other is simply to consider what the writer does with his work in his own playing. Of course, the greatest composers – Ellington, Monk and John Lewis come most rapidly to mind – score on both counts, although it should be emphasised that at present Charles Mingus, jazz's most important orchestral composer after Ellington, belongs largely in the second category.

So does Oscar Peterson. Thus far, he cannot be classed as a major or important composer; but there are signs that writing is beginning to occupy a more central place in his musical life than hitherto. This brief chapter looks at Peterson's achievements in this field so far, and looks forward to two as-yet-unrecorded large projects that may well be available by the time this book is in print.

In Part One I remarked on how uncontroversial Peterson's public persona has always been. But there is nonetheless a profound if dignified radical streak in him, and it emerges most tellingly in his writing. Until recently his best and most famous composition was the gospel-ish blues that closes the *Night Train* album – *Hymn To Freedom*. Its tough but yearning harmonies and its exquisite melody suggest a prayer on behalf of the downtrodden and enslaved everywhere, but of course particularly the Negro.

Peterson has never made an aggressive big deal about his colour. 'I think of myself first and foremost as a human being,' he told Mike Hennessey; and so far as music is concerned, he is comprehensively egalitarian: 'I've always said that talent of any kind comes in a variety of packages – black, white, brown, yellow, tall, short, fat, thin, monster-like or gentle.'[1] In the days of the Herb Ellis group, Oscar was

58

sometimes criticised by fellow-blacks for hiring a white guitarist; Oscar would reply by pointing out, firstly that Ellis was the best possible player for his purposes, and secondly that reverse racial prejudice was no answer to the Negro's problem – Crow Jim was just as bad as Jim Crow. In the same vein, he has expressed impatience with attempts to bring concepts of racial (i.e. black) purity into jazz, finding Leroi Jones's attitudinizing worthless because of its fundamental musical ignorance.[2]

Nevertheless, his consciousness of his race and heritage is most important to him, as he also revealed to Hennessey; and he spoke out on that occasion about South Africa. Asked if he'd every play segregated audiences, he replied:

> No. I was offered concerts in South Africa for years, with all kinds of guarantees, but I have always turned them down. I can't see the sense in playing there. I know that many artists do make tours there, and I have read Arthur Ashe's reasons for going there.* I know what he's trying to do, and I can see that there are two ways of tackling the racial programme. I might be prepared to go there on an educational programme, but I certainly would not consider going on a straight concert tour.[3]

The intelligent reasonableness of these remarks does not obscure the adamantine rejection of racial prejudice and tyranny; and that is now being reflected in his writing. Oscar is currently working on his *Africa Suite*, which started as an individual song dedicated to the imprisoned South African black nationalist leader Nelson Mandella and his wife Winnie. The project has expanded, and still awaits completion; but two pieces have appeared on record, namely the tribute to Mandella, *Fallen Warrior*, and the evocative *Nigerian Marketplace*. Musically these pieces are more ambitious, in both structure and harmonic texture, than Peterson has written before. The lines are long and muscular, and they make central use of Niels Pedersen's formidable singing power, a compositional feature first evident on the lovely *Night Child* (1978), which Oscar wrote to celebrate the birth of his baby son.

Peterson's earlier writing is less propitious, although in the case of his most significant work so far, the *Canadiana Suite*, there is I think an

---

*A celebrated black tennis player, Ashe won the U.S. Open in 1968 and Wimbledon in 1975. Since retiring, Ashe has involved himself deeply in educational projects for blacks, and in the advancement in general of coloured races' opportunities.

5 Bobby Durham – Oscar Peterson – Sam Jones (Hans Harzheim)

important mitigating reason. Oscar began to premiere the suite, piecemeal at least, from 1963; and it was eventually recorded by Limelight in 1964, with Brown and Thigpen. It is much to be regretted that the performance does not rank among the trio's finest, nor indeed is Oscar at his most commanding. They all play well, naturally; but there is a distinct impression of something being held back, or not yet quite arrived at. I have yet to hear a Peterson performance that could be called tentative; but it is salutary, and somewhat frustrating, to compare the full recorded suite with the subsequent versions of some of its movements. The lyrical *Wheatland* is merely pretty on the Limelight; but on the 1972 MPS *Great Connection*, with Louis Hayes and NHOP, the composition is richly explored, emerging as a tune of great fibre. Similarly, the exciting *Hogtown Blues* is markedly inferior to the solo cut on the 1974 *In Russia*; and there are several later recordings of the exhilarating *Place St Henri* that out-distance the Limelight by a fair margin.

In the BBC's *Omnibus* programme from which I've quoted several times, André Previn expressed a great admiration for the *Canadiana Suite* and cajoled Oscar into playing several of its pieces. Once again, these readings were a considerable advance on the original cuts; and a major clue as to why this is so was elicited when Oscar revealed that the compositions were conceived as piano pieces rather than as songs. For with the exception of the suite's *Marchpast*, which makes pivotal use of Thigpen's drums, one cannot say that the recording was undertaken from a *trio* standpoint. The fact that Oscar's subsequent solo versions of his tunes are more impressive than the original group recordings may hinge on the fact that the material was conceptually designed in that way. Certainly, it seems reasonable to argue that the suite's most felicitous expression would be as a solo work; and I would love to hear Oscar re-record it as such. In any event, a re-recording would be enriching whatever the personnel: now that the compositions have developed within his imagination, I am sure that the latent strength of the material would be properly mined.

There have been many other Peterson tunes and projects. Of the individual tunes, *Hallelujah Time* deserves mention as one of the few compositions to be recorded by another major jazz figure: it is one of the outstanding tracks on the excellent *Woody Herman 1964*, arranged by Nat Pierce and featuring a joyous tenor chase. Recently, Oscar has frequently showcased his *Cakewalk*, a witty and intricately boppish shouter; and *The History Of An Artist* contains seven original blues of impressive range. Of the more substantial works, *City Lights* (not yet recorded) is a full-scale ballet score; *The Silent Partner* is a film score for a movie starring Elliott Gould and Christopher Plummer, and which was recorded in 1979 by a group that included Benny Carter, Milt Jackson and Zoot Sims. And *A Royal Wedding Suite* is an *oeuvre d'occasion* of charm and inventiveness, although it is marginal as a jazz work. But it is the *Easter Suite* – just premièred at the time of writing – that is Oscar's most important writing so far.

The *Easter Suite* was commissioned by London Weekend Television, and received its world première on LWT's *The South Bank Show* on Good Friday, April 20, 1984. Its nine movements portray the Easter story from The Last Supper to the Resurrection; and the first thing to emphasise is that it is a genuine *trio* work, and not just for piano plus rhythm accompaniment. Imaginative use is made of Martin Drew's drums, especially in the movements *Denial* and *The Trial*; and a central focus is afforded the exceptional *cantabile* talents of Niels Pedersen. On *Are You Really The King Of The Jews* Oscar and Niels effect a cogent and intricate dialogue that amounts to a kind of fugue; and at the climax of *Why Hast Thou Forsaken Me* Oscar entrusts the enactment of Christ's giving up the ghost to Pedersen's moving cadenza. Throughout one is not only aware of the integration of the group's *playing*: even more pronounced is the structural integration of the writing – it is a genuine *chamber* opus.

The suite has a number of immediate strengths. Its moods and emotional range movingly reflect the mixture of grief and joy that the Easter passion inspires; its melodies have a formidable instant appeal while remaining rich vehicles for exploration; and its linear unity is authoritative and conceptually satisfying. Moreover, its breadth of idiom is notable: Peterson displays a fine understanding of church music harmony and of classical form as well as various jazz forms.

The *Easter Suite* lasted 32 minutes in its televised performance. It is probable that when Oscar puts it on record, it will be longer, featuring more developed improvisations of the nine movements. Even as it stands, however, it is already his most impressive work as a composer and its achievements make one await the appearance of the *Africa Suite* with added impatience. For until very recently it seemed that Peterson's ultimate reputation would rest almost exclusively on his playing; but now there are major signs that such a judgment would have been premature. On the evidence of the *Easter Suite* and the pieces from the *Africa Suite* premièred so far, Oscar's writing has moved to the centre of his musical stage; and the man who laughingly confessed his laziness as a writer to Peter Clayton in 1974 may be about to emerge as one of jazz's more significant composers.

PART THREE:
THE MUSICAL ACHIEVEMENT

In the previous sections I have traced Peterson's career from its Canadian inception to the present day. Such a chronological approach cannot, however, tell the full story. In the end, the most illuminating and enduring aesthetic judgments derive from a critical stance which, while recognising the importance of historical context, also stands free from it, able to assess the work in question in terms of its own purpose and its pure significance as art.

It seems to me especially important to make this point in a book about a jazz musician. For jazz criticism still suffers from a damaging naivety in both a fondness for an adolescently Romantic view of 'the artist' and an excessive respect for 'innovators'. Oscar Peterson's critical reputation and his 'image' have been twin casualties of this regrettable ethos. As 'an unglamorous cat from an unglamorous northern town (Toronto)',[1] Oscar has fallen foul of the facile cultural philosophy that bedevils much jazz polemic; and the fact that it is not possible to talk of a Peterson 'school' of jazz piano, as one can unarguably refer to a Monk, Powell, or Evans 'school', has greatly reduced his oeuvre in the eyes of those from whom greatness in jazz is indissolubly linked with major status as an innovator.

My own view is that although it is absurd to deny the central importance of such innovators as Armstrong, Ellington, Hawkins, Young, Parker, and Gillespie (to name only an obvious few), it is equally absurd to elevate *originality as such* into a primary criterion. In all art, history does not ask who did it *first*, but who did it *best*; and in attempting a critical evaluation of Peterson's music, I shall be arguing that he has the strongest possible claim to be considered under that latter, more decisive category. I start with an analysis of Oscar's musical relationship to Art Tatum.

(i)
Peterson and Tatum

I'd go to bed at night, and it haunted me that someone could play the piano that well. (AP)

Oscar Peterson on first hearing Art Tatum

I have yet to read an account of Peterson's work in any jazz encyclopedia or full-scale survey that does not place him firmly (and usually lukewarmly) in the category of Tatum's acolytes. As I have intimated several times along the way, I consider such a view neither just nor properly illuminating; and this section attempts, through a modicum of musical analysis, to get the matter of Peterson's pianistic relationship to Tatum into some kind of satisfactory perspective.

Most people are to some degree lazy; and critics are people too, even if some musicians do not always seem inclined to agree! So when a musician like Peterson talks with such awe, affection and admiration about a pianist like Tatum, as he always has, the temptation is to take such remarks at face value, and conclude that Peterson's own style is a direct reflection of Tatum's spell. To succumb to such a temptation may be readily understandable, but it does not make for very impressive criticism; and I contend that there has been less and less excuse for such a categorisation of Oscar's style the further one travels down the thirty-five years of his career.

Let us begin with direct comparisons. To play a Peterson version of a song alongside a Tatum performance of the same tune is invariably a salutary experience, showing that there is little close similarity. The *locus classicus* of this phenomenon is Oscar's declared 'tribute' to Art – the 1962 recording of *Ill Wind*, as compared with Tatum's version of the tune on the *Solo Masterpieces* collection.* On the liner notes to the Peterson recording, Oscar comments: 'It's a musical reminder of the way (Art) would handle this type of thing. We used to discuss this at greath length.' However, twelve years later Peterson, having played this arrangement at André Previn's request, argued a very different case:

> As I was playing that, I was thinking to myself, 'This really isn't Tatum.' You couldn't really say that was Art Tatum's style: it was more my *reaction* to that style. (AP)

*The Peterson is on Verve V-8480, the Tatum on Pablo 2625 703.

There is no doubt in my mind that the second of these two comments is much the more accurate. Even on the first chorus, delivered out of tempo, there is only one run that is bona fide Tatum, occurring at bars 22–24 of the theme statement, just before the bridge. (Peterson went on to reveal to Previn that the run in question was the only Tatum run he could *consciously* play.) The rest of this solo passage may be Tatumesque in a very broad sense – the use of lightning arpeggios, the clusters of densely-harmonised notes, the astonishing pirouetting across the entire range of the piano; but at a more detailed and profound level, it is quite distinct from its dedicatee's methods. It is *Peterson's* licks and familiar approach that dominate, not Tatum's. And when Ray Brown and Ed Thigpen enter, the performance removes itself from Tatum's shadow even more obviously. Brown's surging lines are of a kind that one never encounters on any Tatum performance, partly because Tatum's style would never have enabled a bassist to function so centrally or freely. I return to this point shortly.

There are two even more noteworthy differences. One, the track swings in an *earthy* fashion – something Tatum never did; and two, Oscar's reading is much more focused on the melody than was Tatum's wont. One way of putting it might be that Peterson's version is much *easier* to listen to: although the tune's harmonic structure is richly mined, Oscar and Ray keep the melody in the forefront throughout, and their reading has a logic that is comfortable to follow. Listening to Tatum's solo interpretation of the tune hammers home this point even more forcefully.

Tatum's is, naturally, a stunning performance. It begins with a prelude that has little to do with the tune's melody or harmonies, but which sets up the theme statement enchantingly. Then by the time Art reaches the bridge, he is already into rhythmic variations of a subtle and different kind, now slowing, now accelerating the tempo; and once into the development, he demands the strictest attention as he re-writes harmony and structure at will. To be sure, the melody keeps re-surfacing in dazzling, tantalising snippets; but the constant shifts in tempo and key create a fantastic design that utilises the tune as mere clay. Throughout, despite such total transformation, the tune's under-lying shape is implied, and the pulse is infallible: listening to Tatum invariably requires a metronome, if only to prove that *he's* right and your ears are wrong if you detect a dropped or muddied beat. But in essence Tatum's version is the ultimate in baroque, whereas Peterson

6 Oscar in jovial mood, with JATP musicians on arrival in England, 1953(Melody Maker)

offers a fundamentally Romantic treatment, naked and uncluttered in its impact for all its bravura embellishment.

That last distinction serves as a useful summary of their separate styles as a whole; and it throws into starker relief the lack of insight shown by the normally-incisive Martin Williams, who judged Peterson's version 'a feeble pastiche' of Tatum, inferior in harmonic imagination and woefully lacking in 'pianistic adventure'.[2] Not only does this pillory Peterson for qualities he is not attempting to incorporate into his performance: it blatantly ignores the things Oscar *does* do, and which so clearly illustrate a wide discrepancy in both purpose and execution.

In Chapter Five I stressed Peterson's intelligence and awareness as a group pianist. It would be hard to argue that context as Tatum's metier. He was above all a solo virtuoso; and on many occasions one has the impression that playing with others constricts him, somehow lessens his art. Oscar has related that Tatum, playing *Tea For Two* at an old-style 'piano party', got through four bass players in under three choruses. Bassists as accomplished as Red Callender and Ray Brown himself could not stay with Tatum once he started throwing in those chromatic progressions and lightning changes of key. Oscar and André Previn laughed about it together –

Peterson: Can you imagine being in a group with Art Tatum?

Previn: No. It's difficult for me to imagine being in a *room* with Art Tatum! (AP)

– but underneath such loving awe, there is the implication that Oscar had long ago decided that such an approach was not one he wished to emulate. And it is certainly true that Tatum's few trio records are very much piano plus faithful rhythm support, rather than the close-knit and reciprocally-stimulating groups that Peterson had always had.

The distinction is even more pronounced when considering Tatum's work with other soloists. Significantly Roy Eldridge, who made a hatful of superb albums with Oscar, sounds distinctly unhappy on his meeting with Tatum, and the album is one-sided and unsuccessful. Even the date with Ben Webster, an undoubted gem, drew this comment from the tenorist when recalling the session:

Well, really, I shouldn't have been on that album. Nobody should ever have recorded with Art, because he did everything himself. He could say it all better than anyone that ever played with him, and there was so much inside him that he could never be an accompanist.[3]

Listening to the album yet again, I am struck by the incisiveness of Ben's remarks. For in effect Tatum *solos all the time*: there is no real difference between the lines he plays over bass and drums and those he essays while Ben is playing. Webster handles the situation with triumphant common sense, breathing out his langorous improvisations with an infallible regard for the tunes' own structure, leaving Art to do what he likes underneath, in between, and over his work. It's a marvellous record; but the methodology is highly precarious, and a recipe for chaos in most players' cases. It is instructive to compare it with the several albums Ben cut with Oscar, where every member of the personnel works for each other and is absolutely on top of what's going on.

There can be no doubt that Peterson's awe and immersion in Art's work are genuine. As Benny Green once revealed, Oscar is one of the few musicians of his generation to consider Tatum superior in influence and talent to Parker, much though he admires the altoist. How, then, does one explain this reverence *and* the marked disparity in style evident on so many of their respective recordings?

Discussing American literature, Harold Bloom has written a book tellingly entitled *The Anxiety of Influence*. One of its theses is that young writers have to remove themselves from the ambit of a writer they greatly admire, lest that influence drown their own potential to find something distinct to say. The problem is very similar for young jazz musicians; and Peterson recalls his own solution in terms that virtually echo Bloom's:

> If I'd *just* listened to Tatum, I'd have become much the same as several pianists I know in various parts of the world – Tatum reproductions. I remember hearing a young pianist play *The Man I Love* and *Sweet Lorraine* – both straight Tatum. Now, at that time, Tatum hadn't recorded *I Got Rhythm*; and this pianist couldn't play it. He couldn't play it for the simple reason that he had to wait to see what God was going to say about the tune before he copied it. And that's way I never copied Tatum ... You see, if you admire *any* player that much, and you start emulating him, continually, it will just overwhelm you, and you negate any personal creativity you might have that will come forward. (AP)

In other words, Peterson had to come to terms *internally* with the disorientating experience of hearing Tatum. Gradually he *absorbed* its power and its multitudinous messages, and evolved a style that was his own.

In conclusion, another insight from literary criticism furnishes an ideal model for determining the nature of Tatum's effect upon Oscar and its artistic manifestation. Christopher Ricks has suggested that one can see Milton's greatest achievement as the collected works of Alexander Pope. This strange but brilliantly argued notion traces the overwhelming effect that Milton had on the young poet, which fired him with an awed love of Milton's work in particular and poetry's possibilities in general; and as a result he set about carving his own, independent path towards a comparable excellence. In no way do Pope's poems embody a direct, derivative Miltonic style; but the elder poet's aesthetic ethos and linguistic magnificence are permanent imbuing factors.

A similar case can be put forward concerning Peterson and Tatum. Art's comprehensive mastery of the piano ignited the young Peterson's imagination, and that original revelation continues to underscore all that Peterson does. Yet he does it in a fashion that is stylistically separate, where specific purpose and methods bear little direct resemblance. Just as Pope's verse displays a greater bread-and-butter debt to his Augustan predecessor, Dryden, than to the genius who first stunned him, so Peterson's work evinces in its lines, phrasing and general approach a clearer debt to secondary influences – Powell, Cole, Shearing and Hank Jones – than to the man who simultaneously exhilarated and humiliated him. And for my final section, I now turn to an attempt to summarise the main characteristics of the style Peterson evolved in such a way.

(ii)
The Peterson Style

I remember Oscar Peterson listening to Sonny Stitt, and someone was being kind of critical. He heard a lot of Bird clichés just then, he said. And Oscar said, 'Listen to that – he's taken a lot of Bird clichés, and a lot of Lester Young clichés, and a couple of things of Diz's, and I thought I heard something of mine in there, I'm not sure, and he's just smashed them all together, and God, isn't it gorgeous?' And I really drank to that one.[4]

Maynard Ferguson

Peterson's style has often been termed 'eclectic'. In a jazz context, this adjective is invariably pejorative, implying the cobbling-together of others' ideas into a mish-mash that at best merely approximates an individual personality. 'Eclectic' also goes hand-in-hand with the failure to be a true innovator and major influence on others.

It is true that Peterson's playing employs a wide-ranging vocabulary that perforce makes use of other musicians' work. It is also true that he has not founded an identifiable 'school' of jazz piano. A number of pianists show an extensive knowledge of and response to his work – Ross Tomkins, Monty Alexander, Tony Lee, Eddie Thompson, Bernie Senensky (a Peterson protégé) and Brian Lemon; but it cannot be said that Peterson's style has been directly instrumental in influencing the course of jazz, either in terms of the piano, or the music's genesis as a whole.

In my view the best answer to these observations, if they are levelled as criticisms, is a curt 'So what?'. Peterson's eclecticism is not a cannibalization of others' licks and ideas, but the product of a profound and literate awareness of the roots of jazz and its most creative developments. If his playing displays an equal appreciation of the power of James P. Johnson and the subtle revolution in voicings effected by Bill Evans, that seems to me to be cause for celebration and admiration, not derogation. Peterson's style is arguably one of the most personal in jazz, as instantly recognisable as that of Dizzy Gillespie, Lester Young or Johnny Hodges. And the fact that his music covers such a vast idiomatic span is not best served by the parsimonious term 'eclectic': the word I have used several times during this book, 'encyclopedic' is both more accurate and properly complimentary. As a demonstration of this, I'd like to look briefly at the solo performance of *Sweet Georgia Brown* on the *A Salle Pleyel* album.

The introduction and theme are essentially pre-bop in their approach, except that some of the runs hint at Powell-like figures. These are fully developed in the three choruses following the theme, concentrated in the lower half of the piano and punctuated by boppish left hand at the very bed of the bass clef. Then dazzling stride is beautifully incorporated into the next two choruses, culminating in an astonishing unison passage that, set up by dark chords that dramatically break the rhythm, leads into two boogie-woogie choruses recognisably analogous to the old masters, yet done with a contrary-motion melodic attack that is entirely modern. The piece ends with two choruses which increase the already-ferocious tempo by a third, and signs off with a classic blues cadence.

Sweet Georgia Brown is an astounding performance. It is technically awesome, naturally; but the technique is simply the raw material, not the structure itself. The lines overflow with melody and a rich improvisational logic, offering a mini-encyclopedia of jazz piano styles while retaining an inviolate unity as an individual reading. And so the use of boogie-woogie and stride not only pay homage to Tatum, Waller and Wilson, demonstrating Peterson's pre-bop roots,* but by being woven into a majestic tapestry that is the work of a modernist acquire a fresh and organic force. At all times, too, the interpretation is steeped in the earthy directness of the blues. And if it is among the most forbiddingly accomplished of all Oscar's recordings, the things that characterise it are to be found throughout his oeuvre.

The great innovators in jazz piano each added something central to its vocabulary. Earl Hines was the first to show that the piano could be used in jazz as if it were a horn – hence the term 'trumpet style' to define his radical, liberating use of the flashing right hand. Art Tatum brought a transcendent mastery of the piano's orchestral range that will never be repeated, plus a unique harmonic and rhythmic imagination that both anticipated bop and in some ways surpassed it. Thelonius Monk transformed traditional notions of harmonic structure and 'right' notes,

*As the happiest proof of this, Clark Terry's *Ain't Misbehavin* (Pablo 2312 105) is a treat. An album of Fats Waller's songs, it strongly features Oscar on piano, and his grasp of the style is lovingly masterly.

and also, in his oblique fashion, set new trends in the way melody could be explored. Bud Powell, drawing on Monk and Tatum (and on Parker as well) developed a style that was commandingly original in its mixture of linear exploration and harmonic audacity. And Bill Evans became the idol of a whole generation of pianists for his ability to transform harmony from the *inside* of each chord, and for his outstanding lyricism.

Oscar Peterson learnt from all; and he does it all. Monk is not a pianist he admires;* but he absorbed that maverick's melodic innovations, developing an incisive and fetching way of re-working and exploring a melody: two notable examples are *Maria* from *West Side Story*, and Monk's own *'Round About Midnight*, a solo performance to be found on the *Freedom Song* album. His embodiment of the others' contributions I have already gone into, although it is worth stressing the subtle but momentous effect Evans's work exerted on Peterson's ballad readings. A representative specimen is *Who Can I Turn To* on the first solo album, which Evans himself thought 'gorgeous, perfect'.[5] He has used the cornucopian storehouse of jazz piano achievement as one constituent of his own art: the other major ingredients are his own imagination, an incomparable swinging drive, and a direct earthiness whose appeal is as profound as it is immediate.

Oscar Peterson is one of the handful of jazz stars whose eventual demise will mean the end of a noble and priceless style. Those who find him anonymous and mechanical have not, I suspect, listened to enough of his records, or with sufficient care. His style is straightforwardly Romantic in its vitality, warmth, lyrical strength and aspiration. It is pianistically supreme in its comprehensive intelligence and technical prowess, and profoundly durable in its organic variety. Oscar Peterson is one of the few absolute jazz masters, and he leaves no heirs.

*Peterson has always, however, regarded Monk as 'one of the greatest of all jazz composers'.[6]

Notes

PART ONE: THE MAN

1. Leonard Feather, from *Satchmo To Miles* (Quartet, 1974), p.189
2. Ibid, p.189.
3. Alistair Cooke, 'Humphrey Bogart', *Six Men* (Penguin, 1978), p.136.
4. Nat Hentoff, 'The Verve Story', a regular insertion on recent Verve releases.
5. Mike Hennessey, 'An Interview With Oscar Peterson', *Gallery*, 6/76, p.40.
6. Hampton Hawes, *Raise Up Off Me* (Da Capo, 1979), p.83.
7. Feather, *op cit*, p.194.

PART TWO: THE CAREER

Chapter One

1. On Leonard Feather's sleeve essay to Peterson's *Mellow Mood*, MPS 2384 007.
2. *Downbeat*, 29 September 1949.

Chapter Two

1. Steve Voce, 'It Don't Mean A Thing', *Jazz Journal*, 2/71, p.28.
2. Leonard Feather, 'The New Life of Ray Brown', *Downbeat*, 9 March 1967 p.25.
3. Steve Voce, 'It Don't Mean a Thing', *Jazz Journal*, 3/67, p.24.
4. Voce, *Jazz Journal*, 2/71, pp.28–9.

Chapter Three

1. John McDonough, 'The Norman Granz Story', *Downbeat*, 11/79, p.35.
2. On sleeve-essay to Verve V 8024.
3. Len Lyons, 'Oscar Peterson: Piano Worship', *Downbeat*, 18 December 1975,, p.14.
4. Derrick Stewart-Baxter, *Jazz Journal*, 12/64, p.12.
5. Leonard Feather, *The Book Of Jazz* (Bonanza, 1965), p.130.
6. Mike Hennessey, 'First Bass: An Interview With Ray Brown', *Jazz Journal*, 7/82, p.9.
7. Ibid, p.9.
8. Spoken during his Fairfield Hall, Croydon (UK) concert, 4/66.
9. Quoted on sleeve-essay to *Girl Talk*, MPS 583 719.

Chapter Four

1. Lyons, *op. cit*, p.12.
2. Leonard Feather, 'Granzwagon', from *Satchmo To Miles*, pp.184–5.
3. Quoted on sleeve-essay to *This Is Ray Brown*, Verve UMV 2117.

Chapter Five

1. Voce, *Jazz Journal*, 3/67, p.24.
2. Voce, *Jazz Journal*, 2/71, p.28.
3. On the sleeve-essay to *The Trumpet Summit Meets The Oscar Peterson Big Four*, Pablo 2312 114.
4. Peter Clayton, *The Sounds Of Jazz*, BBC Radio 1, January 1976.

Chapter Six

1. Hennessey, *Gallery* interview, p.39.
2. Lyons, *op.cit*, p.14.
3. Hennessey, *Gallery* interview, p.40.

PART THREE: THE MUSICAL ACHIEVEMENT

1. Feather, 'Oscar', from *Satchmo To Miles*, p.189.
2. Martin Williams, 'Oscar Peterson: A Possible Minority Opinion', *Jazz Journal*, 4/64, p.7.
3. Voce, *Jazz Journal*, 3/67, p.24.
4. Kitty Grime, *Jazz At Ronnie Scott's* (Hale, 1979), p.71.
5. Leonard Feather, *The Encyclopedia of Jazz: The Seventies* (Quartet, 1976), p.23.
6. Leonard Feather, 'Three In One: The Oscar Peterson Trio', *Downbeat*, 17 June 1965, p.19.

A SELECTIVE DISCOGRAPHY

A complete Oscar Peterson discography would comfortably fill all of this book. In this necessarily selective chronological listing I have attempted to include all those performances which I consider Oscar Peterson's best, most representative, or most interesting recordings.

The following abbreviations have been used: (as) alto saxophone; (b) bass; (bs) baritone saxophone; (d) drums; (el-p) electric piano; (f) flute; (g) guitar; (hma) harmonica; (org) organ; (p) piano; (tb) trombone; (tp) trumpet; (vcl) vocal; (vib) vibraphone; (vln) violin. All other instruments are given in full. Locations: FGR (Federal Republic of West Germany); LA (Los Angeles); NYC (New York City).

Numbers cited after each session – e.g. (24) – refer to albums listed by title at the end of the discography. A track marked * denotes a specific reference in the main text.

I would like to thank Tony Middleton for his assistance and advice.

RICHARD PALMER, *Barnack, June 1984*

OSCAR PETERSON TRIO

Oscar Peterson (p); Albert King (b); Mark 'Wilkie' Wilkinson (d) *Montreal, April 17, 1947*
BACK HOME AGAIN IN INDIANA/MARGIE/I SURRENDER DEAR/I DON'T STAND A GHOST OF A CHANCE WITH YOU (1)

Oscar Peterson (p); Auston Roberts (b); Clarence Jones (d) *Montreal, December 15, 1947.*
OSCAR'S BOOGIE/SMILES/STAIRWAY TO THE STARS/POOR BUTTERFLY (1)

Same location, March 1, 1949
OOP-BOP-SH-BAM/SWEET GEORGIA BROWN/SLEEPY TIME GIRL/ROCKIN' IN RHYTHM (1)

Oscar Peterson (p); Ben Johnson (g); Auston Roberts (b) *Montreal, November 14, 1949*
FINE AND DANDY/MY HEART STOOD STILL/SOMEBODY LOVES ME/AT SUNDOWN (1)

OSCAR PETERSON

Oscar Peterson (p); Major Holley (b). *NYC, August 5, 1950*
JUMPIN' WITH SYMPHONY SID*/ROBBINS NEST/TICO TICO/GET HAPPY/SMOKE GETS IN YOUR EYES/DEEP PURPLE/EXACTLY LIKE YOU*/I'LL REMEMBER APRIL (2)

Oscar Peterson (p); Ray Brown (b). *NYC, January 19, 1951*
EASY TO LOVE/TAKING A CHANCE ON LOVE/SQUATTY ROO/AFTER ALL (2)

79

OSCAR PETERSON

Oscar Peterson (p); Ray Brown (b). *Carnegie Hall, NYC, September 16, 1950*
GAI* (3)

Oscar Peterson (p); Barney Kessel (g); Ray Brown (b). *Carnegie Hall, NYC, October 11, 1952.*
SWEET GEORGIA BROWN/TENDERLY*/C JAM BLUES*/SEVEN COME ELEVEN* (3)

Oscar Peterson (p); Herb Ellis (g); Ray Brown (b). *Carnegie Hall, NYC, September 23, 1953.*
LOVE FOR SALE/LOLLOBRIGIDA*/POMPTON TURNPIKE*/SWINGIN' TILL THE GIRLS COME HOME* (3)

Hartford, Conn., September 17, 1954
LOVE FOR SALE/NUAGES/AVALON/COME TO THE MARDI GRAS (3)

Opera House, Chicago, October 2, 1955.
BABY, BABY ALL THE TIME/EASY DOES IT/SUNDAY (3)

Note: (3) also includes titles duplicated on (13)

OSCAR PETERSON QUARTET

Oscar Peterson (p); Barney Kessel (g); Ray Brown (b); Alvin Stoller (d). *NYC, December, 1951.*
THE ASTAIRE BLUES/STOMPIN' AT THE SAVOY/BODY AND SOUL/OH, LADY BE GOOD (4)

JAM SESSION

Charlie Shavers (tp); Benny Carter, Johnny Hodges, Charlie Parker (as); Flip Phillips, Ben Webster (ts); Oscar Peterson (p); Barney Kessel (g); Ray Brown (b); J.C. Heard (d). *LA, June, 1952.*
JAM BLUES*/WHAT IS THIS THING CALLED LOVE/BALLAD MEDLEY/FUNKY BLUES* (5)

LESTER YOUNG QUINTET

Lester Young (ts); Oscar Peterson (p); Barney Kessel (g); Ray Brown (b); J.C. Heard (d). *NYC, August 4, 1952.*
JUST YOU, JUST ME*/TEA FOR TWO/AD LIB BLUES/INDIANA/I CAN'T GET STARTED -1/ON THE SUNNY SIDE OF THE STREET/THERE WILL NEVER BE ANOTHER YOU/ALMOST LIKE BEING IN LOVE (6)
-1 Peterson out

ROY ELDRIDGE QUINTET

Roy Eldridge (tp); Oscar Peterson (org); Barney Kessel (g); Ray Brown (b); J.C. Heard (d). *NYC, December 13, 1952.*
LITTLE JAZZ/WRAP YOUR TROUBLES IN DREAMS/ROY'S RIFF/ROCKIN' CHAIR

Jo Jones (d) replaces J.C. Heard. *NYC, April 1953*
LOVE FOR SALE/THE MAN I LOVE/OSCAR'S ARRANGEMENT/DALE'S WAIL (7)

Roy Eldridge (tp); Oscar Peterson (p); Herb Ellis (g); Ray Brown (b); Alvin Stoller (d). *LA, December 10, 1953.*

SOMEBODY LOVES ME/WILLOW WEEP FOR ME/I CAN'T GET STARTED/WHEN IT'S SLEEPY TIME DOWN SOUTH/DON'T BLAME ME/FEELING A DRAFT/ECHOES OF HARLEM/ WHEN YOUR LOVER HAS GONE (7)

Buddy Rich (d) replaces Alvin Stoller. *NYC, September 14, 1954.*

BLUE MOON/STORMY WEATHER/SWEETHEARTS ON PARADE/A FOGGY DAY/IF I HAD YOU/I ONLY HAVE EYES FOR YOU/SWEET GEORGIA BROWN/THE SONG IS ENDED (7)

JAZZ AT THE PHILHARMONIC

Roy Eldridge, Charlie Shavers (tp); Bill Harris (tb); Benny Carter, Willie Smith (as); Flip Phillips, Ben Webster (ts); Oscar Peterson (p); Herb Ellis (g); Ray Brown (b); J.C. Heard (d). *Carnegie Hall, NYC, September 19, 1953.*
COOL BLUES/THE CHALLENGES (8)

Add Lester Young (ts)
ONE O'CLOCK JUMP

LIONEL HAMPTON QUARTET

Lionel Hampton (vib); Oscar Peterson (p); Ray Brown (b) Buddy Rich (d). *NYC, September 2, 1953.*
STOMPIN' AT THE SAVOY/STARDUST/'S WONDERFUL/SOFT WINDS/AIRMAIL SPECIAL (9)

Same location. April 12, 1954.
THIS CAN'T BE LOVE/LOVE FOR SALE/JUST ONE OF THOSE THINGS/APRIL IN PARIS/ HOW HIGH THE MOON/THAT OLD BLACK MAGIC/BLUES FOR NORMAN (9)

Same location. September 13, 1954.
MIDNIGHT SUN/FLYING HOME/HALLELUJAH (9)

JAZZ AT THE PHILHARMONIC

Oscar Peterson (p); Herb Ellis (g); Ray Brown (b). *Nichegei Theatre, Tokyo. November 18, 1953.*
THAT OLD BLACK MAGIC/TENDERLY/BLUES/ALONE TOGETHER*/SWINGIN' TILL THE GIRLS COME HOME (10)

Note: (10) is a 3-volume LP that includes further J.A.T.P. titles with other musicians.

DIZZY GILLESPIE – STAN GETZ SEXTET

Dizzy Gillespie (tp); Stan Getz (ts); Oscar Peterson (p); Herb Ellis (g); Ray Brown (b); Max Roach (d). *NYC, December 9, 1953.*
GIRL OF MY DREAMS/IT DON'T MEAN A THING IF IT AIN'T GOT THAT SWING/IT'S THE TALK OF THE TOWN/SIBLONEY PART 1/SIBONEY PART 2/EXACTLY LIKE YOU/I LET A SONG GO OUT OF MY HEART/IMPROMPTU (11)

JAZZ AT THE PHILHARMONIC

Roy Eldridge, Dizzy Gillespie (tp); Bill Harris (tb); Flip Phillips (ts); Oscar Peterson (p); Herb Ellis (g); Ray Brown (b); Louie Bellson (d). *Stockholm. February 2, 1955*
LITTLE DAVID/OW/BALLAD MEDLEY: THE MAN I LOVE, I'LL NEVER BE THE SAME, SKYLARK, MY OLD FLAME/BIRKS* (12)

OSCAR PETERSON TRIO

Oscar Peterson (p); Herb Ellis (g); Ray Brown (b). *Stratford, Ontario. August 8, 1956*
FALLING IN LOVE WITH LOVE/HOW ABOUT YOU/FLAMINGO/SWINGIN' ON A STAR/
NOREEN'S NOCTURNE/GYPSY IN MY SOUL/HOW HIGH THE MOON/LOVE YOU MADLY*/
52ND STREET THEME (13)

STUFF SMITH QUINTET

Stuff Smith (vln); Oscar Peterson (p); Barney Kessel (g); Ray Brown (b); Alvin Stoller
(d). *LA. February, 1957.*
DESERT SANDS/SOFT WINDS/IT DON'T MEAN A THING IF IT AIN'T GOT THAT SWING/
THINGS AIN'T WHAT THEY USED TO BE/TIME AND AGAIN/I KNOW THAT YOU KNOW
(14)

STAN GETZ QUARTET

Stan Getz (ts); Oscar Peterson (p); Herb Ellis (g); Ray Brown (b). *LA. October 10,
1957.*
I WANT TO BE HAPPY/PENNIES FROM HEAVEN/BALLAD MEDLEY: BEWITCHED
BOTHERED AND BEWILDERED, I DON'T KNOW WHY I JUST DO, HOW LONG HAS THIS
BEEN GOING ON?, I CAN'T GET STARTED, POLKA DOTS AND MOONBEAMS/I'M GLAD
THERE'S YOU/TOUR'S END/I WAS DOING ALL RIGHT/BRONX BLUES (15)

SONNY STITT SEXTET

Roy Eldridge (tp); Sonny Stitt (as); Oscar Peterson (p); Herb Ellis (g); Ray Brown (b);
Stan Levey (d). *LA. October 11, 1957*
THE STRING/CLEVELAND BLUES/B.W. BLUES/BLUES FOR BAGS (16)

COLEMAN HAWKINS – BEN WEBSTER SEXTET

Coleman Hawkins, Ben Webster (ts); Oscar Peterson (p); Herb Ellis (g); Ray Brown
(d); Alvin Stoller (d). *LA. October 16, 1957*
BLUES FOR YOLANDE/MARIA/IT NEVER ENTERED MY MIND/PRISONER OF LOVE/
TANGERINE/LA ROSITA/COCKTAILS FOR TWO/SHINE ON HARVEST MOON/YOU'D BE SO
NICE TO COME HOME TO (17)

JAZZ AT THE PHILHARMONIC

J.J. Johnson (tb); Stan Getz (ts); Oscar Peterson (p); Herb Ellis (g); Ray Brown (b);
Connie Kay (d). *Chicago Opera House. October 19, 1957*
BILLIE'S BOUNCE/MY FUNNY VALENTINE/CRAZY RHYTHM/YESTERDAYS/IT NEVER
ENTERED MY MIND*/BLUES IN THE CLOSET (18)

OSCAR PETERSON TRIO

Oscar Peterson (p); Herb Ellis (g); Ray Brown (b). *Amsterdam Concertge-bauw. March,
1958*
THE LADY IS A TRAMP/WE'LL BE TOGETHER AGAIN/BLUESOLOGY* -1/BUDO/I'VE GOT
THE WORLD ON A STRING/DAAHOUD/WHEN LIGHTS ARE LOW/EVREV (19)

-1 On most commercial issues, "Bluesology" is mistitled as "Bags' Groove"

OSCAR PETERSON TRIO
Oscar Peterson (p); Herb Ellis (g); Ray Brown (b). *Toronto. July, 1958*
SWEET GEORGIA BROWN/SHOULD I/WHEN LIGHTS ARE LOW/EASY LISTENIN' BLUES/
PENNIES FROM HEAVEN/THE CHAMP/MOONLIGHT IN VERMONT (20)

OSCAR PETERSON TRIO
Oscar Peterson (p); Ray Brown (b); Gene Gammage (d). *NYC. November 18, 1958*
ON THE STREET WHERE YOU LIVE/SHOW ME/GET ME TO THE CHURCH ON TIME/I
COULD HAVE DANCED ALL NIGHT/I'VE GROWN ACCUSTOMED TO HER FACE/
WOULDN'T IT BE LOVERLY/THE RAIN IN SPAIN (21)

SONNY STITT QUARTET
Sonny Stitt (as, -1 ts); Oscar Peterson (p); Ray Brown (b); Ed Thigpen (d). *Paris. May 18, 1959*
I CAN'T GIVE YOU ANYTHING BUT LOVE/AU PRIVAVE/THE GYPSY/I'LL REMEMBER
APRIL/SCRAPPLE FROM THE APPLE/MOTEN'S SWING -1/BLUES FOR PRES, SWEETS, BEN,
AND ALL THE OTHER FUNKY ONES -1/EASY DOES IT -1 (22)

OSCAR PETERSON TRIO
Oscar Peterson (p); Ray Brown (b); Ed Thigpen (d). *Chicago. August, 1959.*
DON'T GET AROUND MUCH ANYMORE/SOPHISTICATED LADY/ROCKIN' IN RHYTHM/
PRELUDE TO A KISS/IN A MELLOTONE/COTTONTAIL/JUST A SITTIN' AND A ROCKIN'/
THINGS AIN'T WHAT THEY USED TO BE/TAKE THE 'A'TRAIN/I'VE GOT IT BAD AND THAT
AIN'T GOOD/DO NOTHIN' TILL YOU HEAR FROM ME/JOHN HARDY'S WIFE (23)

BEN WEBSTER QUARTET
Ben Webster (ts); Oscar Peterson (p); Ray Brown (b); Ed Thigpen (d). *NYC. November 6, 1959*
THE TOUCH OF YOUR LIPS/WHEN YOUR LOVER HAS GONE/BYE BYE BLACKBIRD/HOW
DEEP IS THE OCEAN/IN THE WEE SMALL HOURS OF THE MORNING/SUNDAY/THIS
CAN'T BE LOVE (24)

OSCAR PETERSON TRIO
Oscar Peterson (p); Ray Brown (b); Ed Thigpen (d). *NYC. Autumn, 1960*
WHEN DID I FALL IN LOVE/LITTLE TIN BOX/HOME AGAIN/'TIL TOMORROW/POLITICS
AND POKER/GENTLEMAN JIMMY/UNFAIR/ON THE SIDE OF THE ANGELS/WHERE DO I
GO FROM HERE? (25)

OSCAR PETERSON TRIO WITH MILT JACKSON
Milt Jackson (vib); Oscar Peterson (p); Ray Brown (b); Ed Thigpen (d). *NYC. January, 1962*
GREEN DOLPHIN STREET/HEARTSTRINGS/WORK SONG*/JOHN BROWN'S BODY/A
WONDERFUL GUY/REUNION BLUES* (26)

OSCAR PETERSON TRIO
Oscar Peterson (p); Ray Brown (b); Ed Thigpen (d). *NYC. January 24–5, 1962*
SOMETHING'S COMING/SOMEWHERE/JET SONG/TONIGHT/MARIA*/I FEEL PRETTY/
REPRISE (27)

OSCAR PETERSON TRIO WITH THE ERNIE WILKINS ORCHESTRA

Clark Terry, Ernie Royal, Nat Adderley, Roy Eldridge, Snooky Young, Jimmy Nottingham (tp); Jimmy Cleveland, Melba Liston, Paul Faulise, Slide Hampton, Britt Woodman (tb); Willie Ruff, Ray Alonge, Julius Watkins, Morris Secon, Jim Buffington (french horns); Don Butterfield (tuba); Julian 'Cannonball' Adderley (as); James Moody (as, f); Norris Turney, Seldon Powell (ts); Jerome Richardson (bs, f, piccolo); Oscar Peterson (p); Ray Brown (b); Ed Thigpen (d). Arranged and conducted by Ernie Wilkins. *NYC. June 1962*

BLUES FOR BIG SCOTIA/WEST COAST BLUES/HERE'S THAT RAINY DAY/I LOVE YOU/ DAAHOUD/TRICOTISM/I'M OLD FASHIONED/YOUNG AND FOOLISH/MANTECA (28)

OSCAR PETERSON TRIO

Oscar Peterson (p); Ray Brown (b); Ed Thigpen (d). *Chicago. September 25-27, 1962*

WALTZ FOR DEBBIE/TANGERINE/GRAVY WALTZ/THIS COULD BE THE START OF SOMETHING BIG/BAUBLES BANGLES AND BEADS/SIX AND FOUR/I'M A FOOL TO WANT YOU/YOURS IS MY HEART ALONE (29)

OSCAR PETERSON TRIO

Oscar Peterson (p); Ray Brown (b); Ed Thigpen (d). *LA. December 15-16, 1962*
NIGHT TRAIN*/C JAM BLUES*/GEORGIA ON MY MIND*/BAGS' GROOVE*/MOTEN'S SWING/EASY DOES IT*/THE HONEYDRIPPER/THINGS AIN'T WHAT THEY USED TO BE*/ I'VE GOT IT BAD AND THAT AIN'T GOOD*/BAND CALL*/HYMN TO FREEDOM* (30)

OSCAR PETERSON TRIO

Oscar Peterson (p); Ray Brown (b); Ed Thigpen (d). *London House, Chicago. Autumn, 1962*

I'VE NEVER BEEN IN LOVE BEFORE/IN THE WEE SMALL HOURS OF THE MORNING/ CHICAGO/THE NIGHT WE CALLED IT A DAY/SOMETIMES I'M HAPPY/WHISPER NOT/ BILLY BOY (31)

TRICTOTISM/ON GREEN DOLPHIN STREET/THAGS' DANCE*/ILL WIND*/KADOTA'S BLUES (32)

PUT ON A HAPPY FACE/OLD FOLKS/WOODY 'N YOU/YESTERDAYS/DIABLO/SOON/THE LONESOME ONE (33)

THERE IS NO GREATER LOVE/I REMEMBER CLIFFORD/AUTUMN LEAVES/BLUES FOR BIG SCOTIA/SWAMP FIRE/I LOVE YOU (34)

OSCAR PETERSON TRIO

Oscar Peterson (p); Ray Brown (b); Ed Thigpen (d). *NYC. February, 1963*
THE STRUT/LET'S FALL IN LOVE/SATIN DOLL/LITTLE RIGHT FOOT/L'IL DARLIN'/FLY ME TO THE MOON/THIS NEARLY WAS MINE/SHINY STOCKINGS/YOU STEPPED OUT OF A DREAM (35)

OSCAR PETERSON TRIO

Oscar Peterson (p); Ray Brown (b); Ed Thigpen (d). *Villingen, FGR. 1963*
AT LONG LAST LOVE/EASY WALKER/TIN TIN DEO/I'VE GOT A CRUSH ON YOU/FOGGY DAY/LIKE SOMEONE IN LOVE (36)

84

OSCAR PETERSON TRIO

Oscar Peterson (p); Ray Brown (b); Ed Thigpen (d). *NYC. Spring 1964*
QUIET NIGHTS OF QUIET STARS (CORCOVADO)/THE DAYS OF WINE AND ROSES/MY ONE
AND ONLY LOVE/PEOPLE/HAVE YOU MET MISS JONES?/YOU LOOK GOOD TO ME*/THE
GIRL FROM IPANEMA/D & E BLUES/TIME AND AGAIN/GOODBYE J.D.* (37)

OSCAR PETERSON TRIO

Oscar Peterson (p); Ray Brown (b); Ed Thigpen (d). *Tokyo. June 6, 1964*
REUNION BLUES/AT LONG LAST LOVE/I REMEMBER CLIFFORD/BAGS' GROOVE*/
MAINDENS OF CADIZ/TANGERINE/LIKE SOMEONE IN LOVE/SATIN DOLL/TRICOTISM/IT
AIN'T NECESSARILY SO/I LOVES YOU PORGY/TONIGHT/FLY ME TO THE MOON/
SOMEWHERE/YOURS IS MY HEART ALONE/HYMN TO FREEDOM (38)

OSCAR PETERSON QUARTET

Clark Terry (tp, flugelhorn -1 vcl); Oscar Peterson (p); Ray Brown (b); Ed Thigpen
(d). *?NYC. August, 1964*
BROTHERHOOD OF MAN/JIM/BLUES FOR SMEDLEY/ROUNDALAY/MUMBLES -1/MACK
THE KNIFE/THEY DIDN'T BELIEVE ME/SQUEAKY'S BLUES/I WANT A LITTLE GIRL/
INCOHERENT BLUES -1 (39)

OSCAR PETERSON TRIO

Oscar Peterson (p); Ray Brown (b); Ed Thigpen (d). *NYC. Autumn, 1964*
BALLAD TO THE EAST/LAURENTIDE WALTZ/PLACE ST. HENRI*/HOGTOWN BLUES*/
BLUES OF THE PRAIRIES/WHEATLAND*/MARCH PAST*/LAND OF THE MISTY GIANT (40)

OSCAR PETERSON TRIO

Oscar Peterson (p); Ray Brown (b); Louis Hayes (d). *NYC. March 12, 1965*
IF I WERE A BELL/STELLA BY STARLIGHT/BOSSA BEGUINE/L'IMPOSSIBLE/I KNOW YOU
OH SO WELL (41)

Villingen, FGR. 1965
ROBBINS NEST (42)

Oscar Peterson (p); Sam Jones (b); Louis Hayes (d). *NYC. April 5, 1966*
BLUES ETUDE/SHELLEY'S WORLD/LET'S FALL IN LOVE/THE SHADOW OF YOUR SMILE
(41)

Villingen, FGR. 1966
I'M IN THE MOOD FOR LOVE (42)

OSCAR PETERSON TRIO

Oscar Peterson (p); Sam Jones (b); Bobby Durham (d). *Villingen, FGR. 1967*
ON A CLEAR DAY/GIRL TALK (42)

WALTZING IS HIP/SATIN DOLL*/OUR LOVE IS HERE TO STAY/SANDY'S BLUES/ALICE IN
WONDERLAND/NOREEN'S NOCTURNE (43)

Same location. 1969
IN A MELLOTONE/NICA'S DREAM/GREEN DOLPHIN STREET/SUMMERTIME/SOMETIMES
I'M HAPPY/WHO CAN I TURN TO (44)

TRAVELLIN' ON/EMILY/QUIET NIGHTS/SAX NO END*/WHEN LIGHTS ARE LOW (45)

OSCAR PETERSON

Oscar Peterson (p). *Villingen, FGR. 1967*
MEDLEY: I CONCENTRATE ON YOU, MOON RIVER (42)

Same location. 1969
SOMEONE TO WATCH OVER ME/PERDIDO*/BODY AND SOUL/WHO CAN I TURN TO*/BYE BYE BLACKBIRD/I SHOULD CARE*/LULU'S BACK IN TOWN/LITTLE GIRL BLUE*/TAKE THE 'A' TRAIN (46)

Same location. November, 1970
GIVE ME THE SIMPLE LIFE/BASIN STREET BLUES/HONEYSUCKLE ROSE*/DANCING ON THE CEILING*/A CHILD IS BORN/IF I SHOULD LOSE YOU/A LITTLE JAZZ EXERCISE*/DJANGO*/JUST A GIGOLO (47)

OSCAR PETERSON QUARTET

Oscar Peterson (p); Herb Ellis (g); Sam Jones (b); Bobby Durham (d). *Villingen, FGR. November 5-6, 1969*
NAPTOWN BLUES/EXACTLY LIKE YOU/DAY BY DAY/HAMP'S BLUES/BLUES FOR H.G./A LOVELY WAY TO SPEND AN EVENING/SEVEN COME ELEVEN (48)

OSCAR PETERSON TRIO

Oscar Peterson (p); Sam Jones (b); Bobby Durham (d). *NYC. January, 1970*
TRISTEZA/NIGHTINGALE/PORGY/TRISTE/YOU STEPPED OUT OF A DREAM/WATCH WHAT HAPPENS/DOWN HERE ON THE GROUND*/FLY ME TO THE MOON (49)

OSCAR PETERSON TRIO

Oscar Peterson (p); George Mraz (b); Ray Price (d). *Villingen, FGR. November 10, 1970*
BLUES FOR MARTHA/GREENSLEEVES/I'M OLD FASHIONED/ALL THE THINGS YOU ARE/ TOO CLOSE FOR COMFORT/THE JAMFS ARE COMING/IT NEVER ENTERED MY MIND/ CAROLINA SHOUT (50)

Same location. November 12-13, 1970
I LOVE YOU/ROCK OF AGES/ONCE UPON A SUMMERTIME/JUST FRIENDS/TEACH ME TONIGHT/THE WINDMILLS OF YOUR MIND/I DIDN'T KNOW WHAT TIME IT WAS/ALL OF YOU (51)

OSCAR PETERSON TRIO

Oscar Peterson (p); Niels-Henning Orsted Pedersen (b); Louis Hayes (d). *Villingen, FGR. Spring, 1972*
YOUNGER THAN SPRINGTIME/WHERE DO WE GO FROM HERE?/SMILE/SOFT WINDS/ SQUEEZE ME/ON THE TRAIL/WHEATLAND* (52)

OSCAR PETERSON

Oscar Peterson (p); Ray Brown (b). *LA. December 27, 1972*
R.B. BLUES/I WISHED ON THE MOON (53) TENDERLY (54)

Add Irving Ashby (g).
YOU CAN DEPEND ON ME/THIS IS WHERE IT'S AT* (53)

Barney Kessel (g) replaces Ashby
OKIE BLUES (53) WES'S TUNE*/MA HE'S MAKING EYES AT ME* (54)

Herb Ellis (g) replaces Kessel
I WANT TO BE HAPPY*/TEXAS BLUES (53) WHEN YOUR LOVER HAS GONE (54)

Oscar Peterson (p); Sam Jones (b); Bobby Durham (d). *L.A. February 14, 1973*
IN A SENTIMENTAL MOOD/GREASY BLUES/SWEETY BLUES (53) FIVE O'CLOCK WHISTLE (54)

Georg Mraz (b) replaces Jones
GAY'S BLUES/THE GOOD LIFE/RICHARD'S ROUND* (53) OLD FOLKS (54)

Oscar Peterson (p); ; Sam Jones (b); Louis Hayes (d). *L.A. May 25, 1974*
MAINSTEM/DON'T GET AROUND MUCH ANY MORE/SWAMP FIRE (53)

Jones and Hayes out
LADY OF THE LAVENDER MIST*

OSCAR PETERSON TRIO

Oscar Peterson (p); Joe Pass (g); Niels-Henning Orsted Pedersen (b). *London House, Chicago. May 16–19, 1973*
BLUES ETUDE/CHICAGO BLUES/EASY LISTENING BLUES/COME SUNDAY -1/SECRET LOVE (55) REUNION BLUES (54)

-1 Peterson & Pedersen out

OSCAR PETERSON

Oscar Peterson (p. *-1* vcl). *Tokyo. January 15, 1974*
SECRET LOVE/MY FOOLISH HEART/IN A SENTIMENTAL MOOD/THIS IS MY NIGHT TO DREAM -1/I WISHED ON THE MOON/TERRY'S TUNE/I LOVE YOU/LOVE IS A SIMPLE THING/TOO MARVELLOUS FOR WORDS -1/IF I HAD YOU/WHAT ARE YOU DOING THE REST OF YOUR LIFE (56)

OSCAR PETERSON

Oscar Peterson (p). *Tallinn, Russia. November 17, 1964*
I GOT IT BAD AND THAT AIN'T GOOD/I CONCENTRATE ON YOU/HOGTOWN BLUES*/PLACE ST. HENRI*/SOMEONE TO WATCH OVER ME (57)

Add Niels-Henning Orsted Pedersen (b)
ON GREEN DOLPHIN STREET/YOU STEPPED OUT OF A DREAM/WAVE/ON THE TRAIL (57)

Add Jake Hanna (d).
TAKE THE 'A' TRAIN/SUMMERTIME/JUST FRIENDS*/(DO YOU KNOW WHAT IT MEANS TO MISS) NEW ORLEANS/I LOVE YOU PORGY/GEORGIA ON MY MIND/L'IL DARLIN'/WATCH WHAT HAPPENS/HALLELUJAH TIME* (57)

OSCAR PETERSON & DIZZY GILLESPIE

Dizzy Gillespie (tp); Oscar Peterson (p). *London. November 28–9, 1974*
CARAVAN*/MOJAMBIQUE/AUTUMN LEAVES/CLOSE YOUR EYES/BLUES FOR BIRD/DIZZY ATMOSPHERE/ALONE TOGETHER/CON ALMA (58) STELLA BY STARLIGHT/NO GREATER LOVE (65)

OSCAR PETERSON – COUNT BASIE QUINTET

Count Basie (p, org); Oscar Peterson (p); Freddie Greene (g); Ray Brown (b); Louie Bellson (d). *LA. December 2, 1974*

BUNS BLUES/THESE FOOLISH THINGS/'RB'/BURNING/EXACTLY LIKE YOU/JUMPIN' AT THE WOODSIDE/LOUIE B./LESTER LEAPS IN/BIG STOCKINGS/S & J BLUES (59)

OSCAR PETERSON & ROY ELDRIDGE

Roy Eldridge (tp); Oscar Peterson (p, org). *LA. December 8, 1974.*

LITTLE JAZZ/SHE'S FUNNY THAT WAY/THE WAY YOU LOOK TONIGHT/SUNDAY/BAD HAT BLUES/BETWEEN THE DEVIL AND THE DEEP BLUE SEA/BLUES FOR CHU (60) CRAZY RHYTHM/SUMMERTIME (65)

OSCAR PETERSON & HARRY EDISON

Harry Edison (tp); Oscar Peterson (p). *LA. December 21, 1974*

EASY LIVING/DAYS OF WINE AND ROSES/GEE BABY AIN'T I GOOD TO YOU/BASIE/MEAN TO ME/SIGNIFY/WILLOW WEEP FOR ME/THE MAN I LOVE/YOU GO TO MY HEAD (61) SATIN DOLL/MAKIN' WHOOPEE (65)

OSCAR PETERSON

Oscar Peterson (p). *Salle Pleyel, Paris. March 17, 1975*

I GOTTA RIGHT TO SING THE BLUES/MIRAGE/TENDERLY*/INDIANA/IT NEVER ENTERED MY MIND/ELLINGTON MEDLEY: TAKE THE 'A' TRAIN, IN A SENTIMENTAL MOOD, SATIN DOLL, LADY OF THE LAVENDER MIST, THINGS AIN'T WHAT THEY USED TO BE*/SWEET GEORGIA BROWN* (62)

Add Joe Pass (g)

STELLA BY STARLIGHT/JUST YOU JUST ME/IF/HONEYSUCKLE ROSE/BLUES FOR BISE/ PLEYEL BIS (62)

Note: (62) also includes solo performances by Pass.

OSCAR PETERSON & CLARK TERRY

Clark Terry (tp); Oscar Peterson (p). *LA. May 18, 1975*

ON A SLOW BOAT TO CHINA/BUT BEAUTIFUL/SHAW NUFF/SATIN DOLL/CHOPS/MAKIN' WHOOPEE/NO FLUGEL BLUES/MACK THE KNIFE (63) DANISH PASTRY/TRUST IN ME (63)

OSCAR PETERSON & JON FADDIS

Jon Faddis (tp); Oscar Peterson (p). *NYC. June 5, 1975*

THINGS AIN'T WHAT THEY USED TO BE/AUTUMN LEAVES/TAKE THE 'A' TRAIN/BLUES FOR BIRKS/SUMMERTIME/LESTER LEAPS IN (64) OAKLAND BLUES (65)

MILT JACKSON QUARTET

Milt Jackson (vib); Oscar Peterson (p); Niels-Henning Orsted Pedersen (b); Mickey Roker (d). *Montreux, Switzerland. July 17, 1975.*

FUNJI MAMA/EVERTHING MUST CHANGE/SPEED BALL/NATURE BOY/STELLA BY STARLIGHT/LIKE SOMEONE IN LOVE/NIGHT MIST BLUES*/MACK THE KNIFE (66)

Note: A further track from this session, SLOW DEATH, *can be found on Pablo 2683 061*

OSCAR PETERSON & JOE PASS

Oscar Peterson (clavichord); Joe Pass (g). *LA. January 26, 1976.*
SUMMERTIME/BESS YOU IS MY WOMAN/MY MAN'S GONE NOW/IT AIN'T NECESSARILY
SO/I LOVES YOU PORGY/I GOT PLENTY OF NOTHIN'/THEY PASS BY SINGIN'/THERE'S A
BOAT DAT'S LEAVIN' SOON FOR NEW YORK/STRAWBERRY WOMAN (67)

OSCAR PETERSON

Oscar Peterson (p); Ray Brown, Niels-Henning Orsted Pedersen (b). *Montreux, Switzerland. July 15, 1977*
THERE IS NO GREATER LOVE/YOU LOOK GOOD TO ME/PEOPLE/REUNION BLUES/
TEACH ME TONIGHT/SWEET GEORGIA BROWN/SOFT WINDS (68)

SARAH VAUGHAN AND HER QUARTET

Sarah Vaughan (vcl); Oscar Peterson (p); Joe Pass (g); Ray Brown (b); Louie Bellson
(d). *LA. April 25, 1978*
I'VE GOT THE WORLD ON A STRING/MIDNIGHT SUN/HOW LONG HAS THIS BEEN GOING
ON?/YOU'RE BLASE/EASY LIVING/MORE THAN YOU KNOW/MY OLD FLAME/TEACH ME
TONIGHT/BODY AND SOUL/WHEN YOUR LOVER HAS GONE (69)

CLARK TERRY SEXTET

Clark Terry (tp, flugelhorn); Chris Woods (as, f); Oscar Peterson (p); Victor Sproles
(b); Billy Hart (d); Johnny Hartman (vcl). *NYC. March 15–16, 1979.*
JITTERBUG WALTZ/YOUR FEET'S TOO BIG/HONEYSUCKLE ROSE/MEAN TO ME/IT'S A
SIN TO TELL A LIE/AIN'T MISBEHAVIN/SQUEEZE ME/BLACK AND BLUE/I CAN'T GIVE
YOU ANYTHING BUT LOVE/THE JOINT IS JUMPIN' (70)

OSCAR PETERSON QUARTET

Oscar Peterson (el-p, -1 p); Joe Pass (g); Niels-Henning Orsted Pedersen (b); Louie
Bellson (d). *Toronto. April 11, 1979.*
SOLAR WINDS/DANCIN' FEET/SOLILOQUY/NIGHT CHILD* -1/CHARLIE/TEENAGER
(71)

OSCAR PETERSON QUARTET

Oscar Peterson (p); Toots Thielemans (hma); Joe Pass (g); Niels-Henning Orsted
Pedersen (b). *The Hague. July 13, 1980*
CARAVAN/STRAIGHT NO CHASER/LIKE SOMEONE IN LOVE/THERE IS NO YOU/YOU
STEPPED OUT OF A DREAM/CITY LIGHTS -1/I'M OLD FASHIONED/A TIME FOR LOVE/
BLUESOLOGY/GOODBYE/THERE IS NO GREATER LOVE (72)

-1 *Thielemans out*

OSCAR PETERSON TRIO

Oscar Peterson (p); Niels-Henning Orsted Pedersen (b); Terry Clark (d). *Montreux, Switzerland. July 16, 1981*
NIGERIAN MARKETPLACE*/AU PRIVAVE/MEDLEY -1: MISTY, WALTZ FOR DEBBIE/
NANCY WITH THE LAUGHING FACE/CAKEWALK*/YOU LOOK GOOD TO ME* (73)

MILT JACKSON QUARTET

Milt Jackson (vib); Oscar Peterson (p); Ray Brown (b); Grady Tate (d). *NYC. November 30, 1981*
AIN'T BUT A FEW OF US LEFT/STUFFY/A TIME FOR LOVE/BODY AND SOUL/IF I SHOULD LOSE YOU/WHAT AM I HERE FOR? (74)

OSCAR PETERSON

Oscar Peterson (p). *Tokyo. February 20, 1982*
ROUND MIDNIGHT*/MEDLEY: WATCH WHAT HAPPENS, WALTZ FOR DEBBIE (75)

Add Joe Pass (g)
MEDLEY: EMILY, TENDERLY (75)

Add Niels-Henning Orsted Pedersen (b); Martin Drew (d).
MEDLEY: HYMN TO FREEDOM, THE FALLEN WARRIOR*/YOU LOOK GOOD TO ME/ MISSISSAUGA RATTLER/NIGERIAN MARKETPLACE (75)

Same location, February 21, 1982
SWEET LORRAINE/NOW'S THE TIME/NIGHTCHILD/CAKEWALK (75)

Note: (75) includes tracks by Pass and Pedersen, solo and in duo.

OSCAR PETERSON – FREDDIE HUBBARD QUINTET

Freddie Hubbard (tp); Oscar Peterson (p); Joe Pass (g); Niels-Henning Orsted Pedersen (b); Martin Drew (d). *LA. May 24, 1982.*
ALL BLUES/THERMO*/WEAVER OF DREAMS/PORTRAIT OF JENNY/TIPPIN' (76)

OSCAR PETERSON & MILT JACKSON

Milt Jackson (vib); Oscar Peterson (p). *NYC. January 20, 1983*
LADY BE GOOD/IF I HAD YOU/LIMEHOUSE BLUES/MISTER BASIE/REUNION BLUES/ MORE THAN YOU KNOW/JUST YOU JUST ME/HERE'S TWO OF THE FEW (77)

DISCOGRAPHICAL CODA

As I've intimated, Oscar Peterson's recorded output is massive; and even the considerably pruned discography I've included might seem so daunting as to be vague, especially to the enthusiast new to Oscar's work. Accordingly, I list below eight individual tracks which might be said to constitute a notional 'Desert Island' selection from his vast oeuvre. Numbers in brackets refer to the sessions cited in the main discography and listed under title above. My choice is taken solely from Oscar Peterson's work as a soloist or as a trio pianist, and is in order of chronology, not preference.

1. *Tenderly* (3)
2. *Love You Madly* (13)
3. *Bluesology* (19)
4. *I Got It Bad And That Ain't Good* (30)
5. *Bags' Groove* (38)
6. *Lady Of The Lavender Mist* (53)
7. *Hallelujah Time* (57)
8. *Sweet Georgia Brown* (62)

Further Listening Suggestions

Paradise Squat (1952) A Count Basie album that includes three tracks with Oscar guesting on piano and organ. (Verve (A) VE-2 2542)

Oscar Peterson Plays Count Basie (1956) A series of tunes associated with the Basie orchestra, featuring the Brown-Ellis trio augmented by Buddy Rich. (Verve (A) V 8092)

Ella and Louis (1956–7) A 3-LP set highlighting the art of two of jazz's greatest vocalists, with exemplary Peterson accompaniment. (Verve (E) 2615 034)

This Is Ray Brown (1956) Features Jerome Richardson on flute, and Peterson on organ on three tracks. Remarkable for the way Oscar keeps in the background and allows it to be Brown's date through and through. (Verve (J) UMV 2117)

Swinging Brass (1960) Oscar fronting a big band; excellent arrangements by Russell Garcia. (Verve (A) V 6119)

The Jazz Soul (1960) Yet another excellent Brown-Thigpen trio date. (Long-deleted English LP, HMV CLP 1429)

With Stephane Grappelli (1973) Two albums NHOP and Kenny Clarke (America 30 AM 6129/6131)

Montreux '75 Peterson Sextet with Toots Thielemans & Milt Jackson (Pablo 2310 747), and with the Trumpet Kings – Terry, Gillespie & Eldridge (Pablo 2310 754)

Montreux '77 Sessions with 'Lockjaw' Davis, Gillespie and Terry (Pablo 2308 2308), Milt Jackson, Terry and Ronnie Scott (Pablo 2308 210) and as part of the Eddie Davis 4 (Pablo 2308 214).

The Paris Concert (1978) With NHOP and Joe Pass (Pablo 2620 112)

The London Concert (1978) With John Heard and Louie Bellson. (Pablo 2620 111)

The Silent Partner (1979) A version of Oscar's film score, with Jackson, Terry, Zoot Sims & Benny Carter. (Pablo 2312 103)

TITLES OF LP'S

as cited in the main discography

Record numbers are prefaced by (A) America, (E) Europe, or (J) Japan. Pablo issue numbers are the same in Europe and America. Basic recommended albums are those printed **in bold type.**

  (1) *I Got Rhythm* (E) RCA FXM1 7233
  (2) *Keyboard* Verve (A) V 2047, (J) MGV 2666
  (3) In Concert Verve (E) 2683 063
  (4) *Oscar Peterson Quartet* (E) Metronome 0040.198
  (5) *Norman Granz Jam Session* Verve (A) VE–2 2523, (E) 2683 043
  (6) *The Genius of Lester Young* Verve (A) V 8144, (E) 2683 058
  (7) *Dale's Wail* (A) Verve VE-2 2531
  (8) *One O'Clock Jump* (E) Verve VRV 1
  (9) *The Jazz Ambassadors* Verve (A) V 8117, (E) 2683 050
(10) *JATP Live At The Nichegei Theatre* Pablo 2620 104
(11) *Diz & Getz* (E) Verve 2610 045
(12) *The Exciting Battle* Pablo 2310 713
(13) At The Stratford Shakespeare Festival Verve (A) MGV 8024
                                                                (E) 2352 079
(14) *Stuff Smith* Verve (A) MGV 8206, (E) 2304 536
(15) *Stan Getz Meets The Oscar Peterson Trio* (E) 2304 440
(16) *Only the Blues* Verve (E) 2683 060, (J) MV 2634
(17) *Blue Saxophones* Verve (A) MGV 8327, (E) 2304 169
(18) *Stan Getz and J. J. Johnson At The Opera House* Verve (A) V 8490
(19) At the Concertgebauw Verve (A) V 8286, (J) MV 2626
(20) *On The Town* Verve (A) MGV 8287, (J) MV 2607
(21) *My Fair Lady* Verve (A) MGV 2119, (E) VSP 15
(22) *Sittin' In* Verve (E) 2683 060, (J) MV 2538
(23) *The Duke Ellington Songbook* (E) Verve 2332 090
(24) Ben Webster Meets Oscar Peterson Verve (E) 2683 023
(25) *Fiorello* Verve (A) MGV 8366, (E) 8171 081
(26) *Very Tall* Verve (A) MGV 8429, (E) 2332 065
(27) *West Side Story* Verve (A) MGV 8454, (E) VSP 16
(28) *Bursting Out With The All Star Big Band* Verve (A) MGV 8476, (E) 2682 008
(29) *Affinity* Verve (A) V 8615, (E) VLP 9035
(30) Night Train Verve (E) 2352 067
(31) *Live from Chicago* Verve (A) V 8420
(32) *The Sound Of The Trio* Verve (A) V 8480, (E) VLP 9023
(33) *Put On A Happy Face* (E) Verve VLP 9146
(34) *Something Warm* Verve (A) V-8681, (E) VLP 9167
(35) *The Oscar Peterson Trio Plays* Verve (A) V 8591, (J) MV 2104
(36) *Action* (E) MPS 20668
(37) *We Get Requests* Verve (A) V 8606, (E) 2352 065
(38) Live in Tokyo (J) Pablo MW 9055/6
(39) *Oscar Peterson Trio Plus One* Mercury (A) 60975, (E) 20030
(40) *Canadiana Suite* (A) Mercury 86010, (E) Limelight LML 4005
(41) *Blues Etude* (E) Emarcy EMS 2-405

(42) *Girl Talk*   (E) MPS/Polydor 583 719
(43) *The Way I Really Play*   (E) MPS/Polydor 583 715
(44) *Mellow Mood*   (E) MPS 2384 007
(45) *Travellin' On*   (E) MPS/Polydor 583 772
(46) *My Favourite Instrument*   (E) MPS/Polydor 583 721
(47) Tracks   (E) MPS 15063
(48) *Hello Herbie*   (E) MPS 20723
(49) *Tristeza On Piano*   (E) MPS 15143
(50) *Another Day*   (E) MPS 15067
(51) *Walking The Line*   (E) MPS 20868
(52) *Great Connection*   (E) MPS 21281
(53) The History Of An Artist   Pablo 2625 702
(54) The History Of An Artist Vol. 2 Pablo 2310 895
(55) *The Trio*   Pablo 2310 701
(56) *Terry's Tune*   Pablo (J) MTF 1008
(57) In Russia   Pablo 2625 711
(58) Oscar Peterson & Dizzy Gillespie   Pablo 2310 740
(59) *Satch and Josh*   Pablo 2310 722
(60) *Oscar Peterson & Roy Eldridge*   Pablo 2310 739
(61) *Oscar Peterson & Harry Edison*   Pablo 2310 741
(62) A Salle Pleyel   Pablo 2657 015
(63) *Oscar Peterson & Clark Terry*   Pablo 2310 742
(64) *Oscar Peterson & Jon Faddis*   Pablo 2310 743
(65) *Jousts*   Pablo 2310 817
(66) *Jackson*   Pablo 2310 753
(67) *Porgy and Bess*   Pablo 2310 779
(68) *Oscar Peterson and The Bassists*   Pablo 2308 213
(69) *How Long Has This Been Going On?*   Pablo 2310 821
(70) *Ain't Misbehavin'*   Pablo 2312 105
(71) *Night Child*   Pablo 2312 108
(72) *Live At Northsea*   Pablo 2620 115
(73) *Nigerian Marketplace*   Pablo D2308 231
(74) *Ain't But A Few Of Us Left*   Pablo 2310 873
(75) *Freedom Song*   Pablo 2640 101
(76) Face to Face   Pablo 2310 876
(77) *Two Of The Few*   Pablo 2310 881

93